S'mores Cookbook

365 Days of Mouthwatering S'mores Recipes Featuring Everything
from Classic Campfire S'mores to Gourmet Twists

Gary Dortch

Table of Content

INTRODUCTION

Welcome to a year-long journey of indulgence and creativity with the "S'mores Cookbook: 365 Days of Mouthwatering S'mores Recipes Featuring Everything from Classic Campfire S'mores to Gourmet Twists." This comprehensive cookbook is your ultimate guide to enjoying the beloved s'mores treat every day of the year, with a diverse array of recipes that cater to every taste and occasion.

The Essence of S'mores: A Timeless Treat

S'mores, with their perfect combination of graham crackers, gooey marshmallows, and rich chocolate, have been a cherished part of campfires and outdoor gatherings for generations. This book takes that classic treat and elevates it with inventive twists and creative variations, ensuring that you can enjoy s'mores in new and exciting ways all year round.

A Recipe for Every Day

In "S'mores Cookbook," you'll find a recipe for every day of the year, making it easy to incorporate s'mores into your daily life. From the familiar comfort of traditional s'mores to extravagant gourmet creations, each recipe is designed to bring joy and satisfaction to your taste buds.

1. **Classic Campfire Favorites:** Relive the magic of campfire s'mores with recipes that highlight the simplicity and nostalgia of the original treat. Enjoy classics like Campfire S'mores and S'mores Rice Krispie Treats that bring the warmth and fun of outdoor adventures right into your kitchen.
2. **Innovative Twists:** Explore new flavors and textures with inventive recipes such as Nutella Stuffed S'more Cookies, Salted Caramel S'mores, and Mexican Chocolate S'mores Quesadilla. These recipes combine the timeless appeal of s'mores with exciting ingredients and techniques to create unique and memorable treats.
3. **Decadent Desserts and Snacks:** From S'mores Cheesecake and S'mores Crème Brulee to S'mores Pancakes and S'mores Milkshakes, this cookbook offers a range of options that turn s'mores into sophisticated desserts and satisfying snacks.
4. **Simple and Quick Treats:** Need a fast and easy s'mores fix? Discover recipes for Microwave S'mores, No-Bake S'mores Cheesecake, and S'mores Cookie-Dough Truffles that are perfect for busy days when you crave a sweet treat without the hassle.

Elevate Your S'mores Experience

This book is more than just a collection of recipes—it's a celebration of creativity in the kitchen. Whether you're hosting a party, looking for a fun family activity, or simply indulging in a personal treat, "S'mores Cookbook" provides endless inspiration to make s'mores a delightful part of your culinary repertoire.

Each recipe is crafted to balance simplicity with sophistication, making it accessible for both novice bakers and seasoned chefs. The step-by-step instructions and helpful tips ensure that every creation is as delicious as it is enjoyable to make.

Join the S'mores Revolution

With "S'mores Cookbook," you're not just making s'mores—you're experiencing them in a whole new light. Discover how versatile this beloved treat can be and embrace the sweet, gooey joy of s'mores in every month of the year. Get ready to embark on a delicious adventure where s'mores are always the star.

Whether you're revisiting a classic favorite or trying something new, this cookbook is your go-to source for all things s'mores. So gather your ingredients, preheat your oven, and get ready to enjoy 365 days of mouthwatering s'mores recipes that will make every day a little sweeter!

1. CANDIED BACON S'MORES

Prep Time: 5 Mins

Cook Time: 15 Mins

Total Time: 20 Mins

Serving: 1

Ingredients

- 2 slices bacon
- 1 tbsp packed light brown sugar
- graham crackers
- large marshmallow
- Nutella or your favorite hazelnut spread

Directions

1. Set the oven's temperature to 350. Place the bacon on an aluminum foil-covered baking sheet. Evenly sprinkle brown sugar on top of the bacon.
2. Let the bacon cool. Cut into small pieces and store or place in ziplock bags for subsequent assembly.
3. Drizzle graham crackers with hazelnut spread. Place chunks of bacon on top of the crackers.
4. Melt and softly caramelize marshmallows by grilling, roasting over a campfire, or over a flame.
5. Place cooked marshmallow on top of bottom crackers with bacon, followed by the last cracker. Enjoy!

2. BACON-WEAVE S'MORES

Prep Time: 15 Mins

Cook Time: 45 Mins

Total Time: 1 Hr

Serving: 2

Ingredients

- 12 bacon slices, halved
- 2 tbsp. brown sugar
- 6 large marshmallows
- 2 bars chocolate

Directions

1. First, preheat oven to 400ºF. Then, place a baking rack inside a baking sheet to catch oil.
2. Make a bacon weave: Place three bacon halves side by side on the oven rack. Raise one corner of the center bacon slice, then slide a fourth half below and on top of the side pieces. Reposition the center slice.
3. After that, lift the two bacon strips on the sides and lay the fifth bacon half underneath the sides and on top of the central piece. Reposition the side slices.
4. Lastly, raise the opposite end of the central slice and position the sixth slice below the main slice and on top of the side pieces. Repeat to weave three more times.
5. After adding brown sugar to the bacon weaves, bake for 25-35 minutes, till the bacon is crispy. Transfer to paper towel-lined plate to absorb oil.
6. Put three marshmallows on a skewer and cook for two to three minutes, until the marshmallows turn golden.
7. Place marshmallows and chocolate between two bacon weaves.

3. COOKIE BUTTER S'MORES BARS

Prep Time: 30 Mins

Cook Time: 30 Mins

Cool Time: 1 Hr

Total Time: 2 Hr

Serving: 16

Ingredients

Blondie bars

- 14 Lotus cookies
- ½ cup of butter browned
- ¾ cup of brown sugar
- 1 large egg
- 1 tsp vanilla extract
- 1 cup of all-purpose flour
- ½ tsp baking powder
- ⅓ tsp fine sea salt
- ½ cup of white chocolate chips
- 1 cup of cookie butter

Meringue topping

- 2 large egg whites
- ½ cup of sugar
- ¼ tsp cream of tartar
- ½ tsp vanilla extract

Instructions

For the blondies

1. Set the oven's temperature to 350°F. Press parchment paper into an 8 × 8-inch square pan, and then press lotus biscuits onto the pan's bottom.
2. Melt the butter. Melt butter over a medium-high heat source. Cook for a few minutes, periodically turning the pan to avoid scorching. Suddenly, the butter will begin to bubble up and emit a nutty scent. Additionally, you will see that it will begin

to become brown. After that, remove from heat and give it a good swirl. Take caution, as it will immediately begin to brown.

3. Whisk together the butter and brown sugar after adding them. Mix all of the brown butter fragments into the blend. Transfer the mixture to a heat-resistant bowl.

4. Whisk in the vanilla and eggs until glossy and creamy. Next, mix flour, baking powder, and salt using a silicon spatula. Add the white chocolate chips and fold.

5. Evenly spread the batter over the Lotus cookies in the baking sheet. For 23–26 minutes, bake. Spread cookie butter over the cooled blondies.

For the meringue topping

6. Mix the egg whites, sugar, and cream of tartar together in a large heat-safe bowl. Set the bowl over a pot of water that is just barely boiling. (about two inches) over medium heat. Keep the egg bowl's bottom away from the water. Whisk the eggs and sugar together for about 4 minutes until the sugar has dissolved and reaches 160°F. The liquid will thin out and get foamy after first being thick and sticky. Pour the heated egg mixture into a stand mixer with an attached whisk attachment, then stir in the vanilla bean paste. Mix at high speed for 4-5 minutes, until firm, glossy peaks appear. Place a mound of meringue over the cooled brownies, swirling it beautifully. Serve immediately OR use a cooking torch to toast the marshmallow topping for a delectable touch. (Avoid placing it under the broiler in the oven; it will melt.)

4. GRILLED BERRY S'MORES

Total Time: 15 Mins

Serving: 6

Ingredients

- 24 blueberries
- 6 strawberries, stems removed
- 12 large marshmallows
- 12 graham cracker squares
- 3 (1–1.55 oz) chocolate bars, split in half

Instructions

1. Set a grill's temperature to medium.
2. Put two metal skewers with six marshmallows each, six strawberries on one, and twenty-four blueberries on another.
3. Put the skewers with the blueberries and strawberries on the grill.

4. Grill for three to four minutes over medium heat, turning once. Once done, remove from grill and put aside.
5. Top 6 graham cracker halves with 6 chocolate squares.
6. Place the chocolate-topped graham crackers on top of the set if you have a Smores grilling kit. The chocolate-topped graham crackers can be placed on a piece of foil on top rack of the grill, away from direct heat, if you don't have the grilling kit.
7. After the chocolate starts to melt, leave them on the grill for three to four minutes.
8. Arrange the skewers of marshmallows on the grilling set's side. Simply hold the marshmallows over the grill on a skewer for three to four minutes, rotating them regularly, until they are gently browned, if you do not have a grilling set.
9. Top the chocolate-covered graham cracker with one grilled strawberry and four grilled blueberries. Next, top with two toasty marshmallows. Finally, sandwich with another graham cracker square and enjoy!

5. FRUIT S'MORES

Total Time: 15 Mins

Serving: 10

Ingredients

- 1 cup of fresh strawberries
- 1 cup of fresh blackberries
- 1 cup of fresh blueberries
- Graham crackers
- Star shaped chocolate graham crackers
- Large marshmallows
- Hershey's chocolate bar

Instructions

1. First, collect and get ready the ingredients for your s'mores.
2. I prefer to swiftly and efficiently complete this procedure by unwrapping everything and arranging my ingredients. This makes it much simpler for me to grab each meal item as I need it.
3. After that, arrange the tools you'll need for this endeavour so they're easily accessible. Put a few chocolate graham crackers, also known as chocolate graham stars, on a platter or serving tray, then place a couple of the chocolate bars on top of each.

4. Next, place a marshmallow on one of the roasting sticks and very gently toast and brown it with the kitchen torch.
5. You can do a few of these at once if you know how to use a kitchen torch well, but I wouldn't suggest it for people just starting out.
6. Place the marshmallow onto one of the chocolate bars as soon as it's done, then top it right away with the fresh berries.
7. Repeat until all of the fruity s'mores are ready to serve!

6. STRAWBERRY S'MORES

Prep Time: 5 Mins

Cook Time: 5 Mins

Total Time: 10 Mins

Serving: 1

Ingredients

- 1-pint sliced strawberries
- 8 large marshmallows
- 8 Graham Crackers, halved
- 2 chocolate bars, divided

Instructions

1. Slice and clean the strawberries. Place everything in order on the tray or counter.
2. Roast marshmallows until golden and gooey, or to the desired char level.
3. Place two to four chocolate squares on one side of a Graham cracker, top with the marshmallow, put cut berries on top, then cover with another Graham cracker to assemble the marshmallow.

7. BERRIES AND CREAM S'MORES

Total Time: 10 Mins

Serving: 1

Ingredients

- graham crackers (1 cracker per s'more)
- marshmallows (1 mallow per s'more)
- white chocolate (2 pieces per s'more)
- strawberries (sliced)
- raspberries

Instructions

1. Grill the marshmallow until it turns golden brown.
2. Split the graham cracker in half lengthwise.
3. Place two chocolate pieces on one side of your graham cracker, followed by a few strawberry and raspberry slices. Finally, place a toasted marshmallow on top of the second graham cracker.

8. SALTED CARAMEL S'MORES

Prep Time: 20 Mins

Total Time: 55 Mins

Serving: 12

Ingredients

- 1 cup of softened unsalted butter
- ½ cup of packed light brown sugar
- 2 tbsp unsulphured molasses
- 2 tbsp honey
- 1¾ cups of whole-wheat pastry flour
- ¾ cup of all-purpose flour + more for work surface
- 2 tsp ground cinnamon
- 1 tsp kosher salt
- 12 (½-ounce) semisweet chocolate squares
- 12 marshmallows
- 1 cup of salted caramel sauce

Directions

1. First, preheat oven to 325°F and adjust the racks to the top and lower third positions. Whisk the butter, brown sugar, molasses, and honey on medium-high speed for three to four minutes in a stand mixer with paddle attachment till foamy. Stir in whole-wheat pastry flour, cinnamon, all-purpose flour, and salt. Beat at low speed until barely integrated, for about 1 minute, scraping down the edges of the bowl as needed.
2. On a floured surface, roll out the dough to a thickness of roughly ¼ inch. Take a fork and make all over pricks. Cut into 24 (2 ½ inch) squares, then reroll any scraps. Carefully place the dough pieces on two baking pans covered with parchment paper.
3. After that, bake for 15-20 minutes in a preheated oven, rotating the baking pans halfway through to caramelize the edges. Let baking sheets cool for twenty minutes.
4. Set the oven to broil, and place the rack six inches from the heat source. Spread 12 graham crackers on a large baking sheet. Place a chocolate piece and a marshmallow on top of each cracker. Preheat the oven to broil for 1-2 minutes, until the marshmallows are browned. (Alternatively, roast marshmallows over a bonfire or in a kitchen torch until browned.) Drizzle with caramel sauce evenly, and then top with the remaining 12 graham crackers.

9. SMOKED SALTED CARAMEL S'MORES

Prep Time: 5 Mins

Cook Time: 5 Mins

Total Time: 10 Mins

Serving: 4

Ingredients

- 1 package of honey graham crackers
- 4 marshmallows
- 1 bar of caramel-filled milk chocolate
- smoked salt

Instructions

1. Split a graham cracker in half, then top one of the pieces with a couple squares of caramel chocolate.
2. Drizzle a little amount of smoky salt over the chocolate.

3. Toast a marshmallow by placing it over the flame.
4. Place the marshmallow on top of the salted chocolate when it has puffed up and turned golden brown. Press down with the second half of the graham cracker. Enjoy!

10. SAMOA S'MORES

Total Time: 10 Mins

Serving: 4

Ingredients

- 8 large marshmallows
- 16 caramel coconut cookies

Directions

1. Toast marshmallows over an open flame, such as a campfire or your stove, using a stick or skewer. Top one cookie with a toasted marshmallow, then cover with another cookie. Enjoy!

11. HOMEMADE SAMOA COOKIES

Prep Time: 15 Mins

Cook Time: 15 Mins

Additional Time: 30 Mins

Total Time: 1 Hr

Serving: 4 Dozen

Ingredients

- 2 cups of softened butter
- 1 cup of white sugar
- 1 tsp salt
- 4 cups of all-purpose flour, divided
- 1 large egg, lightly beaten
- 2 tbsp vanilla extract
- 1 tsp milk
- 4 cups of sweetened flaked coconut

- 22 ounces caramels
- 1-pound chocolate

Directions

1. Combine butter, white sugar, and salt in a bowl. Mix in 2 cups of flour. Mix add 1 cup of flour and beat until a sticky dough form.
2. Whisk the egg, milk, and vanilla essence together in a bowl. Beat in the remaining flour and egg mixture to make dough. Next, cover bowl with plastic wrap and refrigerate for half an hour.
3. After that, set oven's temperature to 350° F (175° C). Put parchment paper on a baking pan.
4. Roll a small piece of dough into a ¼-inch-thick circle on a lightly floured board. Arrange the circle on the baking sheet that has been prepared. Continue with the leftover dough.
5. Preheat the oven and bake the cookies for 8-10 minutes, until they are soft and golden. Now put cookies on a wire rack to cool all the way down.
6. Cook and stir coconut in a large pan over medium heat till golden brown and toasted, about 2-4 minutes.
7. Whisk the caramel bits around in a bowl that can go in the microwave every 30 seconds for about 2 minutes, until they are smooth and melted. Add coconut to caramel and stir. Place a dollop of the caramel-coconut mixture on top of every cookie.

12. NUTELLA STUFFED S'MORE COOKIES

Prep Time: 30 Mins

Cook Time: 15 Mins

Total Time: 45 Mins

Serving: 12

Ingredients

- 1¾ cups of all - purpose flour
- 1 cup of graham cracker crumbs
- 1 tsp baking soda
- ½ tsp salt
- 1 cup of (2 sticks) softened unsalted butter
- ¾ cup of granulated sugar
- ¾ cup of brown sugar
- 2 tsp vanilla extract
- 2 eggs
- 12 large marshmallows
- 1 cup of chocolate chips
- Nutella for filling

Instructions

1. Silpat mats or parchment paper can be used to line baking sheets. Mix the flour, graham crackers, baking soda, and salt in a separate bowl.
2. Whisk the sugars and butter together in a stand mixer until frothy. Whisk in vanilla and egg until well mixed. Pour in the flour mixture. Add the chocolate chunks and stir. Refrigerate the dough for an hour.
3. Set oven temperature to 375ºF.
4. Scoop out approximately 2 tbsp of dough, then flatten it in your palm. Put one tsp of Nutella in the center. Squeeze the marshmallow gently to make it more compact after placing it on top of the Nutella. Add another scoop of cookie dough on top, and then use your palm to press the rest of the dough into the marshmallow and Nutella until they are fully sealed inside. Place the balls on the cookie sheet and proceed with the leftover dough, spacing them approximately 2 inches apart.
5. Bake till golden, about 15 minutes, then take out of the oven. The marshmallow will first puff up in the cookies, causing them to be uneven, but it will settle back down as they cool. Serve when still a little warm.

13. MEXICAN CHOCOLATE S'MORES QUESADILLA

Prep Time: 15 Mins

Cook Time: 10 Mins

Total Time: 25 Mins

Serving: 6

Ingredients

- 12 street tacos flour tortillas
- 6 tbsp chocolate hazelnut spread
- 1 tsp granulated sugar
- ¼ tsp each ground cinnamon and cayenne pepper
- ½ cup of mini marshmallows
- ½ cup of mini dark chocolate chips
- ½ cup of crumbled shortbread cookies
- 2 tbsp butter

Instructions

1. Spread 1 tbsp of chocolate hazelnut spread equally on 6 tortillas, leaving a 1-inch border all around. Mix the sugar, cinnamon, and cayenne pepper together and evenly distribute them over the chocolate-hazelnut spread. Add chocolate chips, shortbread biscuits, and marshmallows on top. Cover with the remaining tortillas, gently pressing them together.
2. Dissolve half of the butter in a large pan over medium-low heat. Cook the quesadillas, one at a time, for one to two minutes on each side, till they're golden and the filling starts to ooze. If necessary, add the rest of the butter.
3. Slice into wedges and serve right away.

14. CHOCOLATE DIPPED PRETZEL S'MORES

Prep Time: 5 Mins

Total Time: 20 Mins

Serving: 9

Ingredients

- 18 pretzels
- 27 mini marshmallows
- 9 squares of milk chocolate bar
- 1 cup of chopped chocolate
- Sprinkles

Instructions

1. Put nine pretzels in a row on a baking sheet. Place three little marshmallows on top of each. Toast in the broiler.
2. Place a chocolate square on top of each. Turn off the broiler and keep the pan in the oven until the chocolate melts. Place another pretzel on top of each. Allow to solidify (if time is of the essence, freeze it).
3. Microwave the chopped chocolate until it becomes smooth and thin enough to dip S'mores into, stirring every 30 seconds. When the pretzels are solid enough, immerse them in the chocolate with a fork. Tap off the excess chocolate and return it to the pan. Put the S'more on wax paper to set after adding any desired sprinkles.

15. PRETZEL S'MORES BITES

Total Time: 30 Mins

Serving: 46

Ingredients

- 23 large marshmallows, cut in half
- 92 twist pretzels
- 4 milk chocolate candy bars (1.55oz)
- 1 bag semi-sweet chocolate chips

Instructions

1. Place baking paper on a baking sheet. Place 23 pretzels evenly on a baking pan. Place a marshmallow and a slice of Hershey's Milk Chocolate on top of every pretzel. Put under the broiler in the oven and cook until the chocolate softens and the marshmallows start to brown. Take out of the oven and place a pretzel on top of each to make a sandwich. Place in the fridge to solidify the chocolate.
2. Put the metal bowl over a pan of barely boiling water and melt the chocolate chips in it. Remove from heat and stir periodically until smooth. Put each pretzel on the baking sheet after dipping it halfway in molten chocolate. Refrigerate until the chocolate solidifies.

16. S'MORES RICE KRISPIE TREATS

Prep Time: 15 Mins

Cook Time: 5 Mins

Total Time: 20 Mins

Serving: 24

Ingredients

- 6 cups of Rice Krispies Cereal
- 1 bag (10.5-oz) miniature marshmallows
- ¼ cup of unsalted butter
- 1 and ½ cups of graham cracker pieces
- ¾ cup of mini or regular size chocolate chips

Instructions

1. First, spray an 11×7-inch baking pan with nonstick spray. Set aside.
2. Dissolve the butter in a large saucepan. Add the marshmallows and whisk continually until the marshmallows and butter are melted.
3. Take out the pan from heat and add the rice krispie cereal and graham cracker pieces. Blend well.
4. Add chocolate chips and mix just enough to combine them; you want the majority of the chips to stay mostly intact. Press rice krispie treats into the prepared baking pan. Spoon the nonstick spray over the flat side of a spatula and press down to uniformly flatten the rice krispie treats.

5. Chill for about 25 minutes, and then cut into 24 pieces. Cut your treats after 25 minutes in the fridge if they are still too cold. Let them sit on the counter for a few minutes before cutting. I use a serrated knife soaked in warm water to precisely cut squares.

17. S'MORES CRISPY RICE TREATS

Prep Time: 30 Mins

Total Time: 1 Hr

Serving: 6

Ingredients

- One 10-ounce bag mini marshmallows
- One 10-ounce bag bittersweet chocolate chips
- 2 cups of crushed graham crackers
- Nonstick cooking spray, for the pan
- 3 tbsp unsalted butter
- 6 cups of crispy rice cereal

Instructions

1. Set aside ½ cup of crumbled graham crackers, ¾ cup of chocolate chips, and 1 cup of marshmallows to decorate the treats.
2. Lightly coat a metal 8-inch square baking pan with nonstick cooking spray. Cut an 8-inch-wide piece of parchment paper and line the pan, allowing enough overhang on the edges to allow you to pull the goodies out using the flaps. Lightly coat the parchment with nonstick spray.
3. Add the butter to a big, nonstick saucepan and place over medium heat. After swirling until melted, add the marshmallows and stir. It will take around 90 seconds for the marshmallows to melt fully when you gently stir them with a spatula. After taking the pot off of the burner, add the rice cereal and whisk everything together. Add the crushed graham crackers and gently stir in when it has cooled a little. Mix just enough to fold in the chocolate chips; if you stir too much, the chocolate will melt fully.

4. Gently press down on the mixture after pouring it into the prepared pan to ensure that it is distributed evenly. Add the reserved chocolate chips, marshmallows, and crumbled graham crackers while it's still heated. Toast the marshmallows and evenly melt the chocolate with a creme brulee flame, moving in a sweeping manner to prevent the marshmallows from catching fire. This should take around 45 seconds.
5. Let cool fully, approximately half an hour.
6. Cut with a hot, sharp knife into squares and serve.

18. OREO S'MORES BARS

Prep Time: 15 Mins

Cook Time: 20 Mins

Cool Time: 20 Mins

Total Time: 55 Mins

Serving: 6

Ingredients

Crust

- 12 graham crackers
- ¼ cup of granulated sugar
- 24 double stuffed Oreo cookies
- Pinch of salt
- 8 tbsp melted unsalted butter

Topping

- 3 extra-large Hershey bars (about 11 oz), or 7-8 regular-size ones
- 24 jumbo marshmallows

Instructions

1. Set oven temperature to 400°F. Use nonstick spray to lightly oil a 9 by 13-inch baking pan. After that, cover the pan with parchment paper, leaving some hanging over the sides.
2. CRUST: Remove the Oreo cookie tops by twisting them. Put the bottoms (with the cream) aside.

3. Place the graham crackers and the Oreo cookie tops in a food processor and whisk until coarsely crushed.
4. Move the Oreo cookie/graham cracker crumbs to a medium-sized bowl. Mix the salt and sugar into the Graham Cracker crumbs, mixing well. Melt the butter and mix in. Transfer the blend into the ready-made 9x13 pan. Press the crust with your fingertips to form an equal layer.
5. After that, bake for 8-10 minutes, until a light golden color appears around the edges. Take out of the oven and let it 5-8 minutes to cool.
6. TOPPING: Place the chocolate bars on top of the crust, leaving a ¼-inch border of exposed crust visible. Next, place the 24 biscuit bottoms on top of the chocolate bars, cream side up. Top the Oreo cookie bottoms with the marshmallows. The marshmallows will grow in size while they bake.
7. Bake for ten to twelve minutes, or until the marshmallows are golden brown on top and the chocolate is soft.
8. To serve gooey bars, cut them into slices and serve right away.
9. Serving firm bars: After removing from the oven, let them cool for at least 20 minutes.
10. To ensure a gooey texture, microwave individual portions if serving later!

19. SMORES WITH REESE'S CUPS

Total Time: 10 Mins

Serving: 16

Ingredients

- 1 (10 ½ ounce) bag Reese's Peanut Butter cups (large size)
- 16 marshmallows
- 16 graham crackers

Directions

1. Break or split the Graham Crackers into two pieces and put them aside.
2. It's time to warm up the marshmallows. There are a few options for doing this.
3. If you're using a broiler, arrange the marshmallows on top of half of the graham crackers and toast them for a few seconds under the broiler. Take out the Graham and put a Reese's cup on top. Then, put the remaining half of the Graham crack back on top and gently press it to flatten the marshmallows.

4. If you're using a campfire or fire pit, prepare the graham crackers next to the fire and toast them with a tool (such a tree branch or your marshmallow roasting sticks) until they are toasty and golden brown. After placing a Reese's cup on top of half of the graham cracker and a marshmallow on the other half, gently push down to flatten the marshmallows.

5. If using a gas grill or stovetop, prepare the graham crackers next to the burner and toast a marshmallow with a fork (you may use marshmallow roasting sticks or a tree branch). Using the highest heat setting, brown the marshmallow while being cautious not to let it catch fire. Put the browned marshmallow over half of the graham crackers, then top with the remaining graham cracker and Reese's cup. Gently press down to make the marshmallow flat.

20. SNICKERS S'MORES WITH JALAPEÑO

Total Time: 20 Mins

Serving: 10-12

Ingredients

- 1 package of European biscuit cookies
- 3 snickers bars
- 1 package of fresh marshmallows
- 1 jar of pickled jalapenos
- Campfire roasting sticks

Directions

1. Slice the Snickers bars into ¼-inch pieces.
2. Slowly roast your marshmallow until it becomes golden brown and completely melts.
3. Place a biscuit between the toasted marshmallow and two to three Snickers pieces.
4. Place two to three pickled jalapeño slices over the marshmallow and top with another cookie.
5. Before you eat this great treat, let the Snickers melt a bit.

21. SPICY SMOKY S'MORES BARS

Total Time: 30 Mins

Serving: 6

Ingredients

- 2 cups of graham cracker crumbs
- ¼ cup of sugar
- 2 sticks of melted butter
- ½ tsp salt
- 3 cups of chocolate chips
- ½ tsp chipotle pepper powder
- 3 ½ cups of mini-marshmallows

Instructions

1. Set the oven's temperature to 350.
2. Add the salt, sugar, butter, and graham cracker crumbs and mix. Set aside a generous half cup of the mixture. Place the leftover mixture into a 9x13" pan lined with foil. (To remove the bars from the pan for chopping, leave excess foil on the ends.) Bake for ten to twelve minutes. Cool.
3. Melt chocolate over moderate heat in a double boiler. Cover the chilled graham cracker crust with the chipotle pepper powder mixture.
4. Press lightly after scattering marshmallows over the chocolate. Reserving some graham cracker crumbs, press them into the gaps surrounding the marshmallows.
5. Put in the fridge for two hours. Take out of the pan and chop into little squares.

22. S'MORES BAKED OATS

Prep Time: 5 Mins

Cook Time: 25 Mins

Total Time: 30 Mins

Serving: 1

Ingredients

- 1 tbsp flaxseed meal
- 1 ½ tbsp warm water
- ½ cup of rolled or quick oats
- ¼ tsp baking powder
- 2 tbsp cashew butter
- 1 tbsp maple syrup
- ¼ tsp vanilla extract
- ¼ cup of milk of choice
- 2–3 tbsp chocolate chips
- 2 tbsp mini marshmallows
- 1 sheet crushed graham crackers

Instructions

1. Set oven temperature to 350 degrees.
2. First, create the flax "egg" by mixing flaxseed grain and water in a small cup or bowl and letting rest for 5 minutes.
3. Blend the cashew butter, oats, baking powder, maple syrup, flax egg, vanilla, and milk in a blender until a creamy consistency is achieved. Add the chocolate chips and fold.
4. Pour into a greased oven-safe bowl and bake for 20-22 minutes.
5. Take out of the oven, add marshmallows on top, and broil for two minutes.
6. Place a smashed graham cracker on top and savor!

23. MILKY WAY S'MORES GRANOLA BARS

Prep Time: 15 Mins

Cook Time: 15 Mins

Total Time: 30 Mins

Serving: 16

Ingredients

- 6 tbsp unsalted butter
- ¼ cup of packed light brown sugar
- ⅓ cup of maple syrup
- ½ cup of all-purpose flour
- 2 cups of old fashioned oats
- 1 cup of graham cracker crumbs
- ½ tsp salt
- ¼ tsp cinnamon
- 1 cup of roughly chopped Milky Ways
- 1½ cups of mini marshmallows

Instructions

1. Set oven temperature to 350 degrees and coat a 9-by-9-inch baking pan with butter.
2. Mix brown sugar, maple syrup, and butter in a small skillet over medium heat. Spoon the mixture into a large heatproof bowl after the sugar has dissolved.
3. Add the flour, oats, graham cracker crumbs, cinnamon, salt, and stir until the butter mixture coats all of the ingredients.
4. Fill the prepared baking pan with the oat/butter mixture, pressing it firmly.
5. Top with chopped Milky Ways and miniature marshmallows.
6. Granola bars should bake for 15 minutes. Cool in pan and then cut into bars or squares.

24. S'MORES BAKED OATMEAL

Prep Time: 10 Mins

Cook Time: 35 Mins

Total Time: 45 Mins

Serving: 4

Ingredients

- 2 bananas overripe
- ¼ cup of unsweetened applesauce
- 2 tbsp light brown sugar
- 1 tbsp unsweetened cocoa powder
- 1 tsp vanilla extract
- ½ tsp baking powder
- ¼ tsp kosher salt
- 1 cup of unsweetened almond milk
- 1.5 cups of old fashioned oats

Topping

- ½ oz mini marshmallows
- ⅓ oz mini chocolate chips
- 1 tsp graham cracker crumbs

Instructions

1. Set the oven's temperature to 375°F.
2. Coat a small baking dish or casserole with cooking spray. For this, I used an 8.5" x 11" 2.5-quart casserole dish.
3. Mash the bananas with a fork after placing them in the bottom of a mixing bowl.
4. Mix in the applesauce, brown sugar, baking powder, cocoa powder, vanilla extract, and salt.
5. Pour in the milk. Mix thoroughly.
6. Mix the oats. Fold in.
7. Evenly transfer the mixture into the baking dish.
8. After lightly pressing the marshmallows into the oats, sprinkle the topping ingredients over the top.
9. Bake for 35 minutes at 375°F.

25. GOOEY S'MORES BARS

Prep Time: 20 Mins

Total Time: 1 Hr 15 Mins

Serving: 24

Ingredients

- ⅔ cup of sugar
- ½ cup of softened butter or margarine
- ½ tsp vanilla
- 1 egg
- 2⅓ cups of graham cracker crumbs
- ⅓ cup of all-purpose flour
- ⅛ tsp salt
- 1 bag (11.5 oz) milk chocolate chips
- 1 jar (7 oz) marshmallow creme
- 1 cup of miniature marshmallows

Instructions

1. Preheat the oven to 350°F. Coat the 13 x 9-inch pan with cooking spray or shortening to grease the bottom and edges.
2. Lightly whisk the sugar, butter, vanilla, and egg in a big bowl with an electric mixer set at medium speed, or stir with a spoon, until frothy and light. Add the salt, flour, and graham cracker crumbs and stir. Set 2 cups of the graham cracker mixture aside. Press the remaining mixture into the crust-forming pan.
3. Sprinkle chocolate chunks over the crust and press lightly. Drop marshmallow crème by tablespoonfuls over chocolate chips. Wet the back of a crockery spoon and use it to spread marshmallow crème. Add some marshmallows on top. Apply the set-aside crumb mixture and gently press it in.
4. Bake for 17 to 22 minutes, until the marshmallows are lightly golden brown and puffy. Cool for at least 30 minutes. Cut the bars into 6 rows by 4 rows.

26. S'MORES PANCAKES RECIPE

Prep Time: 15 Mins

Cook Time: 20 Mins

Resting Time: 10 Mins

Total Time: 45 Mins

Serving: 2

Ingredients

- 110 g flour
- 10 g cocoa powder
- 30 g sugar
- 10 g baking powder
- ½ tsp salt
- 180 ml full-fat milk
- 1 egg
- 1 tsp vanilla essence
- 30 g melted butter,
- 1 packet large marshmallows, cut in half
- Sweetened whipped cream (for topping)
- Melted chocolate (for topping)
- Crushed graham crackers/digestive biscuits (for topping)

Instructions

1. Combine all dry ingredients: flour, cocoa powder, baking powder, sugar, and salt in a bowl using a hand whisk.
2. In a separate bowl, whisk together your liquid ingredients: full-fat milk, egg, melted butter, and vanilla essence until well combined.
3. Next, pour your liquid ingredients into your dry ingredients and mix them using a hand whisk until there are no streaks of flour visible in the batter. Don't worry if there are a few lumps. Let the batter sit for 10 minutes to improve pancake rise.
4. Set your nonstick pan on low heat when you're ready to cook the pancakes. Make sure the pan is hot before you add the batter.
5. Pour two tbsp batter into the pan, then spread it in a circle. Place 5-6 pieces of marshmallows on top of the batter, then cover them with more batter. Try to cover all the edges of the marshmallow with the batter. Then cover pan with a lid to allow the pancakes to cook evenly without burning the bottom.

6. Let the pancake cook for 3-5 minutes, then carefully run your spatula under it to release it from the pan, flip it, cover and cook again for another 2-3 minutes until it is cooked through. Repeat the process for the remaining pancakes.
7. To serve, stack the pancakes and put a spread of whipped cream, melted chocolate, and crushed graham crackers on top of each one. Enjoy warm.

27. GLUTEN FREE DECADENT S'MORES FRENCH TOAST

Prep Time: 10 Mins

Cook Time: 10 Mins

Total Time: 20 Mins

Serving: 4

Ingredients

- 6 slices gluten-free bread
- 1 egg
- 1½ cups of vanilla oat milk
- ½ tsp cinnamon
- 1 tsp vanilla extract
- 2 tbsp sugar
- 4 tbsp dairy-free butter
- 2 cups of gluten-free graham cracker crumbs
- Dairy-free chocolate spread for topping
- Marshmallow fluff for topping

Instructions

1. Combine the egg, sugar, cinnamon, vanilla, and oat milk well.
2. Transfer the graham cracker crumbs to another bowl.
3. Dip the bread in graham cracker crumbs after dipping it in the egg mixture.
4. Preheat a skillet over medium heat.
5. Add and melt 1 tbsp of butter. Add bread when butter has melted and become heated.
6. Cook around 3 minutes per side. The French toast has to be a rich golden brown.
7. Add marshmallow fluff and chocolate spread to each French toast piece. Enjoy!

28. SAVORY S'MORES

Total Time: 25 Mins

Serving: 15

Ingredients

Herb and Cheese Cookies

- 1 cup plus 2 tbsp all-purpose flour
- 1 tbsp thinly sliced chives
- 2 tsp minced thyme
- 1 tsp minced rosemary
- ½ tsp salt
- ¼ tsp black pepper
- ½ cup of cold unsalted butter, slice into small cubes
- 4 ounces grated Parmesan (about 1 heaping cup)
- 1 tbsp cold water

Assembly

- 6 ounces very thinly sliced prosciutto
- 1-pound brie, cubed into 1 ½ inch squares
- honey for drizzling and serving

Instructions

1. Preheat the oven to 350° F.
2. Put the flour, herbs, salt, and pepper in a bowl and mix them all together with a whisk.
3. Put the Parmesan and butter into the food processor's well and pulse three to four times.
4. After scraping down the bowl's sides, add the flour mixture. Process ingredients until the flour and butter mixture combine to form sloppy dough balls.
5. Add water and pulse 4 to 5 more times.
6. Put the ingredients on a clean, lightly floured surface. Using light strokes, form the dough into a ball.
7. Next, cover dough with plastic wrap and put it in the fridge for an hour.
8. Remove the dough from the refrigerator and set it on a freshly floured board.
9. After that, roll dough to ¼ inch thickness using a rolling pin.

10. Cut out as many cookies as you can with a 2 ½-inch round or fluted circle cookie cutter, then place them approximately 1-inch apart on a baking sheet wrapped with parchment paper.
11. Bake cookies till golden brown, 18 to 22 minutes.
12. Remove the cookies from the oven and lay them on a cooling rack to cool fully.
13. **For S'more:** Preheat broiler to high. Place half of the cookies on a baking sheet, then place a piece of prosciutto on top of each. Place a square of brie on top of each prosciutto slice and broil for 30 seconds to 1 minute, until the rind starts to caramelize and the brie starts to soften but doesn't melt entirely.
14. Take the cookies out of the broiler, cover with honey, and sprinkle the remaining cookies on top. Serve immediately.

29. STOUT-INFUSED MARSHMALLOW & BACON S'MORES

Prep Time: 1 Hr

Total Time: 5 Hr

Serving: 50

Ingredients

- 4 oz bacon
- ½ cup of milk
- 3 packets unflavored gelatin
- 1 ½ cups of sugar
- 1 cup of corn syrup
- 1 tsp vanilla extract
- ¼ cup of cornstarch
- ½ cup of powdered sugar
- dark chocolate granola thins

Instructions

1. First, cook bacon over medium heat to render fat and crisp it up. Transfer the grease and bacon to a food processor. To crumble the bacon, pulse it.
2. Transfer the milk to the food processor and pulse until well mixed. Place the blend in the refrigerator to chill down. It must be faintly solidified once completely chilled. Transfer it to the stand mixer bowl and combine with the gelatin.

3. Put the corn syrup, sugar, and ⅔ cup of water in a saucepan and bring to a candy thermometer's reading. Add the sugar and stir it in constantly until it melts. After bringing to 240°F, stop stirring.
4. Pour the heated sugar mixture into the milk/bacon combination while keeping the mixer on low. Once it has doubled in size and is considerably lighter in color, turn it up and mix on high for approximately 15 minutes.
5. Combine the powdered sugar and cornstarch. Wrap the bottom of a 6 × 9 pan with parchment or plastic. Spoon part of the cornstarch and sugar mixture on top. Pour the marshmallow mixture over the powdered sugar. Add more on top, then cover and chill for about three hours, or until solidified.
6. Cut into 1-inch marshmallows and sprinkle with more sugar-cornstarch mixture just until barely coated.
7. Toast your marshmallows and sandwich them between two granola thins to make s'mores!

30. MARGHERITA S'MORES

Prep Time: 5 Mins

Cook Time: 2 Mins

Total Time: 7 Mins

Serving: 8

Ingredients

- 16 Ritz crackers
- 8 slices mozzarella (vegetarian brand, if required)
- 8 sundried tomatoes
- 8 fresh basil leaves

Instructions

1. Set the grill's temperature to high. Arrange eight Ritz crackers with a piece of mozzarella on top on a baking sheet lined with parchment paper. Grill for 1 minute, until the cheese begins to melt.
2. Add a sun-dried tomato and a basil leaf on the top, then place another Ritz cracker over them.

31. SPICY SALAMI S'MORES

Prep Time: 5 Mins

Cook Time: 2 Mins

Total Time: 7 Mins

Serving: 8

Ingredients

- 16 melba toasts
- 8 slices Taleggio
- 8 slices spicy salami
- 4 black olives, halved

Instructions

1. Preheat the grill to high and prepare a baking sheet with paper. Place 8 melba toasts on a platter, top with a slice of Taleggio, and place under the grill for the cheese to begin melting.
2. Place a black olive, salami, and another melba toast on top.

32. TASTY S'MORES

Prep Time: 5 Mins

Cook Time: 10 Mins

Total Time: 15 Mins

Serving: 4

Ingredients

For Campfire

- 4 whole graham crackers
- 4 marshmallows
- 4 pieces chocolate

For Air Fryer

- 4 whole graham crackers
- 2 marshmallows
- 4 pieces chocolate

Instructions

1. Break all graham crackers in half to make 8 squares. Arrange one chocolate square on four Graham Cracker squares.
2. Put the marshmallows on a roasting stick or skewer. Toasted to your desired texture, either roast over an open flame or grill.
3. Place marshmallow on chocolate-covered graham cracker, then cover with second piece of graham cracker.

For Air Fryer

4. Make eight squares by breaking each graham cracker in half. Cut marshmallows in half crosswise with scissors.
5. Place the marshmallows on four Graham Squares, cut side down. Place the marshmallow side up in the air-fryer basket and cook for 4-5 minutes at 390° until golden.
6. Take out of the air fryer, top each toasted marshmallow with chocolate and a graham cracker, and serve.

33. CAMPFIRE S'MORES

Total Time: 10 Mins

Serving: 1

Ingredients

- 1 graham cracker
- ½ chocolate candy bar
- 1 marshmallow

Instructions

1. Make a fire in your fireplace or a campfire. Instead of having a roaring inferno of flames, let the fire simmer until the logs are only red-hot embers.

2. Cut one long graham cracker in half lengthwise to get two square pieces. Break the chocolate bar into one graham cracker square, leaving the other square open to serve as the top. Set aside.
3. Place a marshmallow on a stick and cook, flipping often, until golden brown (or dark brown or burned, if you choose!) and gooey inside.
4. Take the marshmallow off of the flame and put it over the chocolate. Place the second piece of graham crackers on top of the marshmallow. Enjoy this traditional delight by eating it sandwich style!

34. INDOOR S'MORES

Prep Time: 10 Mins

Cook Time: 5 Mins

Total Time: 15 Mins

Serving: 12

Ingredients

- 12 graham crackers, broken in half
- 12 marshmallows
- 2 Hershey milk chocolate bars, broken into segments

Instructions

1. Preheat broiler and place an oven rack in the highest position. Then, use aluminum foil to cover a baking sheet.
2. Lay out 12 halves of graham crackers on the baking sheet with lining. Put a marshmallow, positioned on its long side, in the middle of each cracker.
3. Broil with the oven door slightly open for 15 to 30 seconds, until the marshmallows are browned to your preference. Keep a watchful eye on them as they may quickly turn from perfectly scorched to burned.
4. Put two pieces of chocolate on top of every marshmallow. Cover with the remaining half of graham crackers and squish everything together. Give the s'mores a few minutes to cool so the chocolate can begin to melt. Enjoy and go in deep!

35. OVEN S'MORES

Prep Time: 2 Mins

Cook Time: 5 Mins

Total Time: 7 Mins

Serving: 4

Ingredients

- 4 sheets of graham crackers
- 1 Hershey chocolate bar
- 4 marshmallows

Instructions

1. Set your oven's broiler on high.
2. Place four half-sheets of graham crackers—or as many you choose to make—on your baking pan.
3. Place three Hershey's chocolate pieces and a marshmallow on each cracker.
4. Put in the broiler for one minute or so. They brown fast, so watch them carefully!
5. Take out of the oven and cover the marshmallows with the remaining half of a cracker.

36. GIANT S'MORES COOKIES

Prep Time: 20 Mins

Cook Time: 15 Mins

Total Time: 35 Mins

Servings: 12

Ingredients

- 2½ cups of all-purpose flour
- 1½ tsp salt
- ¾ cup of graham cracker crumbs
- 1 tsp baking powder
- ¼ tsp baking soda
- 1 cup of cubed unsalted butter cold

- 1¼ cups of light brown sugar packed
- 2 large eggs
- 2½ tsp vanilla extract
- 1 cup of semi-sweet chocolate chips
- 5 bars milk chocolate bars, broken into pieces
- 12 marshmallows large, square
- 1 bar milk chocolate bar to garnish

Instructions

1. Preheat the oven to 375° F. Put parchment paper on one baking sheet and set it aside.
2. Mix the flour, baking powder, baking soda, graham cracker crumbs, and salt together. Set aside.
3. Whisk brown sugar, granulated sugar, and butter for 4-5 minutes on medium-high speed till light and fluffy.
   Note that if you use a manual mixer, this may take an extra minute or two.
4. Add eggs one at a time and stir.
5. Mix in vanilla extract.
6. Stir in the flour mixture gradually.
7. Add the chocolate chips and candy bar bits and mix until well incorporated using a low-speed mixer.
8. After that, roll each chunk of dough into a ball after scooping out ¼ cup (or weighing out 4 oz).
9. Bake only six cookies at a time, spaced widely apart.
10. Next, bake for 15-20 minutes at 375°F in a preheated oven. Puff up and lightly brown the edges.
    TIP: Bake longer for crispier, chewier cookies. Bake them for softer, more gooey cookies.
11. Place cooled cookies on the baking sheet. Move to a rack for cooling.
12. Place a marshmallow in the middle of each biscuit. Toast marshmallows with a cooking torch or broil until golden brown.
13. Put one chocolate candy bar piece in the middle of the heated marshmallow.

37. DEEP DISH S'MORES BOWLS

Total Time: 25 Mins

Servings: 2-4

Ingredients

- 3 tbsp melted butter
- 2 tbsp brown sugar
- 1 tbsp white sugar
- 1 egg yolk
- ¼ tsp vanilla
- ¼ tsp baking powder
- ¼ cup + 1 tbsp flour
- ⅛ tsp salt
- 2 graham cracker sheets, crushed into crumbs
- 8–10 Hershey chocolate squares, or ¼ cup of semisweet chocolate chips
- heaping ½ cup of mini marshmallows

Instructions

1. Set oven temperature to 350. Combine butter, brown sugar, and white sugar. Add vanilla and egg yolk and whisk. Whisk in graham crackers, flour, baking powder, and salt.
2. To prepare the crust, divide the dough between the ramekins (I generally use two, but you may use three or four depending on size). Next add a layer of chocolate on top, and lastly, a generous amount of marshmallows.
3. Bake the marshmallows for 15 minutes, until they are crispy and lightly browned. Cool to your liking, and serve the gooey delight with big spoons and milk.

38. S'MORES BROWNIES

Prep Time: 20 Mins

Cook Time: 15 Mins

Total Time: 35 Mins

Servings: 12

Ingredients

Brownies

- 1 (18.3 ounce) package fudge brownie mix
- ½ cup of vegetable oil
- 2 large eggs
- 3 tbsp water

S'mores Topping

- 6 graham crackers
- 1 ½ cups of miniature marshmallows
- 8 (1.5 ounce) bars coarsely chopped milk chocolate

Directions

1. Preheat your oven to 350° Fahrenheit. Butter a 9 x 13-inch baking pan.
2. Prepare the brownies: Combine the brownie mix, oil, eggs, and water until thoroughly combined in a medium bowl. Transfer the mixture into the ready pan.
3. Bake for fifteen minutes in a preheated oven.
4. Prepare the topping while the brownies are baking: Break the graham crackers into 1-inch pieces and place in a bowl. Toss to mix in the chopped chocolate and marshmallows.
5. Take out brownies from the oven and sprinkle with toppings. Put it back in the oven and bake for another 7 to 10 minutes, until a skewer inserted 2 inches from the pan's edge pulls out clean.

39. GIANT STUFFED S'MORES COOKIES

Prep Time: 15 Mins

Cook Time: 15 Mins

Chill Time: 15 Mins

Total Time: 45 Mins

Servings: 12

Ingredients

- 2 sticks softened salted butter
- ¾ cup of dark brown sugar
- ¼ cup of granulated sugar
- 2 eggs, at room temperature
- 2 tsp vanilla extract
- 2 ¼-2 ⅓ cups of all-purpose flour
- 1 tsp baking soda
- ½ tsp kosher salt
- 1 cup of milk chocolate chips
- ¾ cup of dark chocolate chips
- 12 jumbo marshmallows
- flaky salt, for sprinkling

Instructions

1. Set the oven's temperature to 350. Then, prepare 2 large baking sheets with parchment paper.
2. After that, beat butter and sugars together in a large bowl for two to three minutes, until it's frothy. Add the eggs one at a time, beating until well combined. Mix in the vanilla extract. Mix in the baking soda, salt, and 2 ¼ cups of flour until well blended. After that, prepare 2 large baking sheets with parchment paper. Mix in the chocolate chips, both dark and milk.
3. Form a mound of dough the size of a third of a cup in your hand, then gently press it down to create a depression in the middle. Put the marshmallow in the hole and then fold the dough around it. It's fine if the mallow isn't completely covered. Place dough in the prepared baking tray after rolling it into a cylinder. Proceed with the leftover dough. Put no more than five dough balls onto your baking pans. You might have to work in groups.

4. Put the baking sheets in the freezer for 15 minutes. Take it out and bake for 9 minutes. Press down hard on the edge of the counter with the baking sheets until the centers become flat. Bake for three more minutes, then tap again. Give it one last thump on the counter and bake for another 3 minutes, until the edges are brown and firm. After 10 minutes on the baking pans, transfer the cookies to a wire rack. Warm some and chill the rest.

40. FANCY S'MORES

Total Time: 45 Mins

Servings: 4

Ingredients

- graham crackers
- marshmallows
- variety of fancy chocolates
- salted caramel
- fruit such as bananas, strawberries, blackberries
- almond butter

Instructions

1. Roast marshmallows on a gas burner or over a campfire.
2. Put together the s'mores.
3. Smush and eat!

41. BEST S'MORES SANDWICH

Prep Time: 5 Mins

Cook Time: 10 Mins

Total Time: 15 Mins

Servings: 1

Ingredients

- 2 slices bread
- 2 tbsp Nutella
- 1 tbsp butter
- 1 tbsp crushed graham crackers
- 1 (1.55 oz) bar milk chocolate
- 6 regular-sized marshmallows

Instructions

1. Set an oven rack at 350 degrees Fahrenheit and place a silicone baking mat on the rim of the sheet.
2. On one side of every slice of bread, spread Nutella. Set aside.
3. In a sauté pan or cast-iron skillet, melt butter over medium heat.
4. Toast the bread slices one next to the other, Nutella side facing, until the bottoms are golden brown.
5. Place the bread on prepared baking sheet, side by side.
6. Place graham cracker crumbs (gently pressed into Nutella) on top of one side, followed by chocolate.
7. Top with marshmallows on the other side.
8. Bake for about five minutes in a preheated oven until the marshmallows bubble up and turn brown.
9. Now, keep the baking sheet on the middle rack and broil it to finish browning.
10. Sandwich together, cut, and serve.

42. GRILLED S'MORES SANDWICH

Prep Time: 2 Mins

Cook Time: 3 Mins

Total Time: 5 Mins

Servings: 1

Ingredients

- 2 slices bread
- butter
- milk chocolate chips (or milk chocolate bar)
- 3 large marshmallows

Instructions

1. Heat a frying pan over medium-low heat.
2. Generously butter the bread and arrange one piece of butter side down. Evenly distribute milk chocolate chips on top. Place the marshmallows on top of the chocolate chips after gently squashing them. Place the remaining bread piece, butter side up, on top.
3. Cook for 3–4 minutes on each side, or until melted and brown within!

43. HAZELNUT S'MORES SANDWICH

Prep Time: 5 Mins

Cook Time: 15 Mins

Total Time: 20 Mins

Servings: 8

Ingredients

- 1 (24-inch) baguette, halved lengthwise
- 1 cup of chocolate hazelnut spread
- 1¼ cups of marshmallow creme
- 2 crumbled graham crackers

Directions

1. Set the oven's temperature to 350°. To make a hollow, remove a little portion of the bread's soft inside. Evenly cover one half of the bread halves with the chocolate hazelnut spread, then top with marshmallow cream and graham cracker crumbs. Place the two together and cover with foil. Bake for about 10 minutes, until well warmed.

44. GIMME GIMME S'MORES SANDWICH

Prep Time: 5 Mins

Inactive Time: 1 Hr

Total Time: 1 Hr 5 Mins

Servings: 1

Ingredients

- One sheet of low-fat honey graham crackers (4 crackers)
- ¼ cup of fat-free whipped topping, thawed from frozen
- 1 tsp mini semi-sweet chocolate chips
- 8 miniature marshmallows

Directions

1. Cut the Graham Cracker sheet in half. Set aside.
2. Combine marshmallows, chocolate chips, and whipped topping in a small bowl and whisk gently. Avoid over-stirring.
3. Arrange a square of graham crackers on a platter, then cover with the whipped topping mixture. Place the other square on top very gently.
4. Freeze for approximately 1 hour or until solid. Keep chilled until you're ready to serve. Enjoy!

45. PEANUT BUTTER S'MORES SANDWICH

Total Time: 10 Mins

Servings: 1

Ingredients

- 1 tbsp creamy peanut butter
- 1 slice crusty white bread
- 1 tbsp milk chocolate chips
- 2 tbsp miniature marshmallows

Directions

1. Toast the toast with peanut butter on it. Transfer to a baking sheet and garnish with marshmallows and chocolate chips. Now broil 4–5 inches from the heat source for 30–60 seconds, until it's gently browned.

46. S'MORES ICE CREAM SANDWICHES

Prep Time: 10 Mins

Chill Time: 30 Mins

Total Time: 40 Mins

Servings: 4

Ingredients

- 4 graham crackers
- 4 tbsp hot fudge topping
- 4 corner marshmallows
- 4 small scoops vanilla bean ice cream

Instructions

1. Cut the Graham Crackers in half lengthwise to get eight squares.
2. Place four squares of graham cracker on a dish, smooth back side up. Over each square, distribute 1 tbsp of hot fudge topping. While toasting the marshmallows, place the platter in the freezer to set.

3. Roast the Corner Marshmallows while the fudge is freezing. You may use a blow torch, an oven, or a skewer over a fire or gas burner to do this. When use the oven, Arrange the marshmallows on the final four graham crackers and arrange them on a parchment paper-lined baking sheet. Bake for 5 minutes at 400°F, till the marshmallows are lusciously gooey and golden brown.
4. Place each marshmallow on the smooth side of one of the leftover graham crackers and set them away once they are toasted.
5. Remove the fudge-filled graham crackers from the freezer. Add ice cream to the fudge using a spoon or tiny scoop. Take care not to overdo it or your sandwiches will become quite sloppy.
6. Press down hard to sandwich together the graham cracker with marshmallow on top of the ice cream.
7. Place in the freezer for at least a half hour or until ready to serve! Devour!

47. S'MORES WAFFLE SANDWICH

Prep Time: 10 Mins

Cook Time: 10 Mins

Total Time: 20 Mins

Servings: 4-6

Ingredients

- Waffle batter
- 1 bag of marshmallows
- 1 cup of graham cracker crumbs
- 1 cup of milk chocolate chips

Instructions

1. Prepare waffles as directed on the package. Line up on wax paper.
2. When the meal is finished, preheat the waffle iron, set half of the waffle inside, and prepare the other half for folding over. Top with ¼ cup of milk chocolate chips, ¼ graham cracker crumbs, and marshmallows. Close the iron after pressing down the second side of the waffle. Cook until marshmallow is flowing out and chocolate begins to melt.

48 S'MORE SANDWICH COOKIES

Total Time: 50 Mins

Servings: 12

Ingredients

- 1 (16 oz) package of refrigerated chocolate chip cookie dough
- 2 cups of powdered sugar
- 1 (7-oz.) jar marshmallow creme

Instructions

1. Bake cookies as indicated on the package. Give it ten minutes or so to cool fully.
2. Meanwhile, whisk marshmallow cream and ½ cup of powdered sugar in a medium bowl.
3. Whisk in remaining 1½ cups of powdered sugar on a surface dusted with powdered sugar. Make two 12-inch ropes out of the mixture. Cut ropes into lengths of two inches. Put one piece between two cookies and push them together lightly. Continue with the remaining biscuits and marshmallow fragments.

49. S'MORES GRILLED CHEESE

Total Time: 40 Mins

Servings: 4

Ingredients

- 2 slices white bread
- 1 tbsp butter
- ¾ cup of graham cracker crumbs
- 4 tbsp marshmallow fluff
- 4 tbsp chocolate hazelnut spread
- 2 tbsp mascarpone cheese

Directions

1. Set a skillet over medium heat.
2. Crumble graham cracker crumbs onto a dish. Drizzle each slice of bread with butter on one side, then place it on top of the graham cracker crumbs butter side down.

3. Spread mascarpone cheese and then chocolate hazelnut spread on one slice of bread each. Place a layer of marshmallow fluff on the second slice of bread. Gently place the two pieces together so that the marshmallow fluff and chocolate meet in the center. If necessary, add additional graham cracker crumbs to the bread.
4. Now place sandwich in the warm skillet and cook for about 2 minutes, till the bread is toasted and golden. Grill for another two minutes after flipping the sandwich. Remove and enjoy!

50. FROZEN S'MORES

Prep Time: 20 Mins

Freezing Time: 6 Hr

Total Time: 20 Mins

Servings: 15

Ingredients

- 1 box instant chocolate pudding
- 2.5 cups of cold milk
- 16 graham crackers
- 7 oz marshmallow creme
- 4 oz softened cream cheese
- 8 oz frozen whipped topping thawed

Instructions

1. Cover a 9x13 pan with foil or parchment paper, leaving extra paper to hang over the edges.
2. Mix pudding mix and milk in a medium-sized bowl until well combined and creamy. Transfer into a 9x13 pan and level the surface.
3. Chill the pudding layer while you prepare the marshmallow layer.
4. Whisk the marshmallow cream and cream cheese together in a medium-sized bowl until smooth. Add the whipped topping and fold.
5. Cover the chocolate layer with the marshmallow layer. Cover with foil.
6. Freeze layers for about 6 hours, until solid enough to cut through. Place the 9x13 pan on a chopping board after removing the layers using foil or parchment paper.
7. Halve fifteen graham crackers. Cut the pudding/marshmallow layers into fifteen identical-sized squares, much like the graham crackers. If your layers have frozen very firm, wait 15 minutes before slicing.

8. Place layers of food between two Graham Cracker pieces. (For a simple method to accomplish this, view the video in the post.)
9. Eat immediately away or freeze sandwiches in an airtight bag or container. I find that the flavors are enhanced when the graham crackers are frozen for a time and then softened somewhat. For the greatest texture, let them come to room temperature for 15 to 20 minutes after freezing.

51. CAMPFIRE SMORES RECIPES

Prep Time: 1 Min

Cook Time: 2 Mins

Total Time: 3 Mins

Servings: 1

Ingredients

- 1 graham cracker split in half
- ¾ oz. milk chocolate candy bar, about ½ of a single serving
- 1 marshmallow

Instructions

1. Get your campfire going.
2. Place marshmallow on roasting stick.
3. Toast marshmallow over campfire flames to desired level.
4. Place marshmallow and chocolate bar between split graham cracker to make sandwich.

52. PUMPKIN S'MORES BARS

Prep Time: 25 Mins

Total Time: 1 Hr 16 Mins

Servings: 1

Ingredients

- Nonstick cooking spray
- 8 finely crushed graham crackers, whole sheets
- ½ cup plus 2 tbsp. brown sugar
- 4 tbsp. melted unsalted butter (½ stick)
- 15 oz. 100% pure pumpkin
- 12 oz. evaporated milk
- 2 large eggs
- 1 tsp. ground cinnamon
- ½ tsp. ground ginger
- ¼ tsp. salt
- 1 cup of semisweet chocolate chips
- 1¼ cups of mini marshmallows

Instructions

1. Preheat your oven to 350°F. Cover the sides of a 9-inch square baking dish with aluminium foil, allowing it to hang over the edges by approximately 2 inches. Coat the foil with cooking spray.
2. Press butter, two tbsp brown sugar, and broken graham crackers firmly into the bottom of the prepared dish using a medium bowl. Bake for ten minutes, until the crust is lightly browned; cool on a wire rack.
3. After that, combine the remaining ½ cup of brown sugar, pumpkin, milk, eggs, salt, cinnamon, and ginger in a large bowl. Then, whisk in the ½ cup of chocolate chips. Cover the crust with the pumpkin mixture and top with remaining ½ cup of chocolate chips. Bake for 50 minutes, until the center is almost set and a knife inserted one inch from the edge of the dish comes out clean. Refrigerate for a minimum of three hours or up to overnight after cooling for thirty minutes on a wire rack.

4. Adjust the broiler to high and place the oven rack six inches from heat source. Place marshmallows on the bar and toast them for 30 seconds in the broiler until they turn golden brown. Lift the bar out of the dish and place it on a cutting board by using the foil's overhanging edges. Cut into 16 squares after removing the foil. Keep bars refrigerated for up to a week in an airtight container.

53. S'MORES DESSERT PIZZA RECIPE

Prep Time: 15 Mins

Cook Time: 10 Mins

Total Time: 25 Mins

Servings: 8

Ingredients

- Pizza dough store bought or homemade
- ⅓ cup of brown sugar
- ½ cup of rolled oats
- 2 tbsp softened butter
- ¼ cup of flour
- 1 bag mini marshmallows
- 1 bag semi-sweet chocolate chips

Instructions

1. Prepare the dough according to the directions.
2. After that, combine butter, brown sugar, and flour in a medium-sized bowl. Mix with a fork until it resembles cornmeal.
3. Add the rolled oats. Blend well.
4. Evenly distribute ingredients over prepared pizza dough.
5. Top pizza with chocolate chips.
6. Over the chocolate chips, generously scatter marshmallows.
7. Bake pizza dough according to the recipe or directions. (Note: If the crust takes longer than ten minutes to cook, wait and add the marshmallows until the pizza is approximately ten minutes from done. That keeps them from becoming overly heated.)

54. S'MORES COOKIE SANDWICH

Prep Time: 13 Mins

Cook Time: 8 Mins

Total Time: 21 Mins

Servings: 18

Ingredients

- ½ cup of softened butter
- ½ cup of peanut butter creamy
- ¾ cup of granulated sugar divided
- ½ cup of brown sugar
- 1 egg large
- 1 tsp vanilla extract
- ½ tsp baking soda
- 1¼ cups of all-purpose flour
- ½ tsp baking powder
- 7 ounces marshmallow fluff
- ½ cup of semi-sweet chocolate chips
- ½ cup of heavy whipping cream

Instructions

1. Set the oven to 375° Fahrenheit and line baking pans with parchment paper.
2. Cream peanut butter and softened butter with a large stand mixer or by hand. Scrape down the sides of the bowl as necessary. Add ½ cup of sugar, egg, and cream. Beat for two to three minutes until it's light and fluffy.
3. Combine cream, vanilla, and brown sugar.
4. Separately, mix the baking soda, baking powder, and flour in a different bowl.
5. Mix butter mixture with the flour mixture until well combined.
6. Make use of a size 24 medium cookie scoop. Spread the cookie dough out on the baking sheet 2 inches apart and coat each piece with the extra sugar.
7. Make hash marks in the dough with the back of a fork, allowing the cookie dough to spread a little.
8. Turn fork 90 degrees, then set hash marks on top to form a crisscross.
9. Bake till the edges are golden brown, 7 to 9 minutes at 375 degrees. Avoid overbaking.
10. Take out of the oven and let cool for one minute on the pan.
11. Next, place biscuits on a cooling rack to cool completely.

12. Apply marshmallow fluff to eighteen cookies.

13. Toast marshmallow fluff for one to two minutes in the oven under the broiler.

14. After that, mix chocolate chips and heavy cream in a separate bowl. Heat in microwave for 30 seconds, then whisk. Stir until smooth and heat for another 15 seconds.

15. Cover the toasted marshmallow fluff with chocolate ganache and place a cookie on top.

16. Cookies may be kept for up to a week in the refrigerator in a sealed container. Enjoyed best within two to three days.

55. CHOCOLATE CHIP GRAHAM CRACKER S'MORES SANDWICH COOKIES

Total Time: 30 Mins

Servings: 12

Ingredients

- ½ cup of softened butter
- ¾ cup of light brown sugar
- ¼ cup of granulated sugar
- 1 tsp vanilla extract
- 1 egg
- 2 cups of ground graham cracker crumbs, divided
- ¾ cup of all-purpose flour
- ½ tsp baking soda
- ¼ tsp salt
- 1¼ cups of chocolate chips
- ¾ cup of marshmallow fluff
- 10 ounces chopped and melted good quality chocolate

Instructions

1. Preheat the oven to 350° Fahrenheit. Then, whisk butter, brown sugar, and granulated sugar in the bowl of your stand mixer till frothy and light. Mix in egg and vanilla essence until thoroughly blended.

2. Mix 1 ½ cups of graham cracker crumbs, baking soda, flour, and salt in a medium-sized bowl. Gradually add dry ingredients, mixing until just mixed. Add the chocolate chunks and stir.

3. Place dough balls the size of cookies—roughly 24 in total—on baking pans, and bake for nine to ten minutes. Take out of the oven and allow it to cool down a little bit on the cookie sheets before moving it to cooling racks.

4. Combine similar-sized and shaped cookies once they have cooled. Spread approximately 1 tbsp of fluff on the bottom of one cookie from each pair. Place the second cookie on top of the sandwich, then continue with the additional cookies.

5. Place sandwich cookies on a dish covered with wax paper after dipping them halfway into chocolate. Sprinkle the leftover smashed graham crackers on top right away. Before eating, let the chocolate firm entirely.

56. S'MORES SUGAR COOKIE SANDWICHES

Prep Time: 30 Mins

Cook Time: 8 Mins

Total Time: 38 Mins

Servings: 10

Ingredients

Cookie

- 1¼ cups of flour
- ¼ cup of crushed graham crackers
- ½ tsp baking soda
- ¼ tsp salt
- ⅛ tsp cinnamon
- ¼ cup of melted unsalted butter
- ¼ cup of oil
- ½ cup of granulated sugar easy baking tub
- ½ cup of dark brown sugar
- 1 large egg, at room temperature
- 1 tsp vanilla extract

Chocolate

- 1 cup of semi-sweet chocolate
- ½ cup of heavy whipping cream
- marshmallow meringue

- 3 large egg whites
- ¾ cup of dark brown sugar
- 1 tsp vanilla extract

Instructions

1. Mix the flour, baking soda, crumbled graham crackers, salt, and cinnamon in a medium-sized bowl. Put the dry ingredients into a separate container.
2. Melt the butter in a big dish and mix in the oil, Dark Brown Sugar, and Easy Baking Tub Granulated Sugar. Blend the blend until it's well blended. After adding the egg and vanilla essence, stir the mixture until it is fully smooth.
3. Add the dry ingredients and fold only until the last flour streak is integrated. Set aside to cool while you have the oven preheated to 350 degrees. Then scoop cookie dough onto a prepared cookie sheet using a 1 tbsp cookie scooper. Bake six cookies at a time, spaced about three to four inches apart, for eight minutes, until the edges begin to crisp. Although they may appear undercooked, take them out of the oven and give them five more minutes to finish baking on the cookie sheet. Taking off the cookie sheet, put it on the cooling rack.

Make the chocolate

4. Transfer the chocolate chips to a medium-sized, heat-resistant bowl. Fill a small pot with the heavy whipping cream and place it over low heat. When it's simmering, pour it over the chocolate, wait a minute or two, and then stir gently until the mixture is smooth. After a few minutes of cooling, spoon some onto half of the cookies.

Make the marshmallow meringue

5. In the meanwhile, put a small pot over low heat with ½ cup of water. To make a double boiler, put the bowl of a stand mixer over the small saucepan and add the egg whites and Dark Brown Sugar. In order to completely dissolve the Dark Brown Sugar, cook the egg whites for 5 to 10 minutes. After taking the bowl from the stove, mix it on high speed for seven minutes using a stand mixer. Mix in vanilla essence just until smooth. Melancholy frost the remaining half of the cookies with a piping bag (or a spoon). Place the cookies one on top of the other.
6. You can serve the cookies right away, but put them in the fridge for a few hours to keep the meringue from spreading out.

57. S'MORES BANANA SANDWICH MELT

Total Time: 20 Mins

Servings: 4

Ingredients

- 8 slices bread
- ½ cup of Nutella
- 2 peeled and sliced bananas
- 1 cup of mini marshmallows
- 2 tbsp softened butter

Instructions

1. First, butter one side of each slice of bread. Flip the bread over and add 1 tbsp Nutella on each. Divide the prepared bread into half and set aside.
2. Place the sliced banana on the side of the remaining 4 pieces of bread with Nutella. Evenly distribute two tbsp of marshmallows. With the buttered side facing up, stack with the prepared bread that was set aside to make a sandwich.
3. Over medium heat, preheat a nonstick pan or griddle. Place the sandwiches on the pan and cook for two to three minutes or until golden brown. After flipping, cook the opposite side until golden brown and the marshmallows and Nutella start to melt. Remove from heat and serve.

58. DEEP-FRIED NUTELLA S'MORES SANDWICH

Total Time: 20 Mins

Servings: 2

Ingredients

- 2 pieces white bread
- 1 tbsp Nutella
- 1 tbsp marshmallow cream
- 1 cup of Bisquick mix + ¼ -½ cup of water (batter needs to be thick)
- As needed, Chocolate syrup to drizzle

Instructions

1. Preheat the fryer to 375°.
2. Sandwich one slice of bread with Nutella and the other with marshmallow cream, then assemble.
3. Coat in batter and cook for three to five minutes, until it's golden brown.
4. Slice on the diagonal, then pour syrup over it. Serve warm.

59. HIGH-PROTEIN PEANUT BUTTER S'MORES COOKIE

Total Time: 30 Mins

Servings: 6

Ingredients

- 25 g oat flour (blended oats)
- 12 g slow-release casein - vanilla
- 12 g powdered peanut butter
- 2 g baking powder
- 30 g fat-free Greek yoghurt
- 30 ml unsweetened almond milk
- 3 g sugar-free maple syrup
- a few drops FlavDrops
- 5 g mini dark chocolate chips
- 5 g sugar-free marshmallows

Instructions

1. Set oven temperature to 180°C.
2. Whisk the flour, peanut butter, flour, and baking powder together in a mixing bowl.
3. Then, combine your almond milk, maple syrup, Greek yogurt, and FlavDrops in a bowl and whisk to form a cookie dough. Add your marshmallows after that.
4. Add your chocolate chips and shape the batter into cookies using a 5-inch skillet or a baking sheet after it is workable by hand.
5. Put in the oven at 180°C for 4 minutes and 45 seconds. Let it cool before eating. Ice cream is optional.

60. CHARCOAL-CARAMELISED S'MORES

Prep Time: 15 Mins

Cook Time: 10 Mins

Total Time: 25 Mins

Serving: 20

Ingredients

- 150 g plain savory crackers
- 150 g mini marshmallows
- 50 g chopped and melted dark chocolate

Instructions

1. Place the chocolate in a double-boiler.
2. Permit the chocolate to trickle down one side of each biscuit after dipping it along one edge. Transfer to a platter and let the chocolate harden.
3. Place a marshmallow on top of each biscuit when the chocolate has solidified. Using a pair of tongs, gently push a hot piece of charcoal onto the marshmallow.
4. Take off the charcoal as soon as the marshmallow tops are caramelized, then serve right away.

61. S'MORES CREME BRULEE

Prep Time: 30 Mins

Bake: 25 Mins + Chilling

Cook Time: 55 Mins

Serving: 6

Ingredients

- 1 cup of 2% milk
- 3 large eggs, room temperature
- ⅔ cup of sugar
- ⅓ cup of baking cocoa
- 2 tbsp coffee liqueur
- ⅔ cup of graham cracker crumbs
- 2 tbsp butter, melted
- ⅓ cup of sugar
- 2 cups of miniature marshmallows
- 1 milk chocolate candy bar (1.55 oz), broken into 12 pieces

Directions

1. Turn the oven on at 325°. Remove from heat after heating milk in a small saucepan until bubbles start to form around the pan's edges. Whisk together the eggs, sugar, cocoa, and liqueur in a large bowl until well combined but not frothy. Whisk in the heated milk slowly.
2. Six 4-ounce broiler-safe ramekins should be placed on a baking pan big enough to accommodate them all without touching. Fill ramekins with egg mixture. Set pan on oven rack and fill pan with very hot water to ½ inch over ramekins. A knife placed in the middle should come out clean after baking for 20 to 25 minutes, although the centers will still be mushy. After removing the ramekins from the water bath, let them cool for ten minutes on a wire rack. Put in the fridge to get cold.
3. Combine butter and cracker crumbs in a small bowl and put it aside. Sprinkle sugar evenly over custards and use a cooking flame to caramelize the topping. Hold the torch flame approximately two inches above the custard surface, then slowly rotate it so the sugar caramelizes evenly. Crumble mixture over custards and place

marshmallows on top. Toast marshmallows with a torch until browned. Add some chocolate chunks on top. It can be served right away or chilled for up to an hour.

4. Note: Place the ramekins on a baking sheet and let them stand at room temperature for 15 minutes to caramelize the topping under a broiler. Warm up the broiler. Evenly sprinkle sugar over custards. Allow the sugar to caramelize for 3–4 inches under the broiler for 3–5 minutes. Crumble mixture over custards and place marshmallows on top. Allow marshmallows to brown for 30 to 45 seconds under the broiler. Add some chocolate chunks on top. Serve right away or chill for up to an hour.

62. S'MORES CHEESECAKE

Prep Time: 40 Mins

Total Time: 6 Hrs 20 Mins

Serving: 16

Ingredients

Crust

- 1¼ cups of graham cracker crumbs
- 3 tbsp granulated sugar
- ¼ cup plus 2 tbsp butter, melted

Cheesecake

- 3 packages (8 oz each) soften cream cheese
- 1 cup of packed light brown sugar
- ⅓ cup of marshmallow creme
- 1 tbsp vanilla
- 4 eggs
- ¼ tsp ground cinnamon
- 1 cup of milk chocolate chips (6 oz)

Topping

- 1 cup of milk chocolate chips (6 oz)
- ¼ cup of whipping (heavy) cream

Instructions

1. Preheat the oven to 425°F. Then, coat a 10-inch springform pan with cooking spray.
2. After that, combine all crust ingredients in a small bowl. Take out and save ½ cup of the mixture for topping. Evenly press the leftover mixture into the pan's bottom. Bake for five minutes, or until the crust's edges are beginning to become a deep golden color.
3. Smooth out cream cheese in a large bowl by using an electric mixer on medium-speed and stopping to scrape the sides every so often. Beat in vanilla, marshmallow creme, and brown sugar until smooth. Beat for 1 minute after adding each egg one at a time. With a rubber spatula, mix in the cinnamon. Cover crust with 1 cup of chocolate chips. Cover chips with batter.
4. Bake cheesecake for 15 minutes at 225°F in the oven. Bake for an additional 55 minutes, or until the cheesecake is almost set in the center but still somewhat jiggly around the edges. (Never test doneness with a knife; the hole might cause the cheesecake to split.) After turning off the oven, slightly open the door and let the cheesecake come to room temperature. Take out of the oven, cover loosely with foil, and chill for a minimum of three hours.
5. Melt 1 cup of chocolate chips and the whipping cream in a 1-quart pan over low heat, stirring from time to time. Scatter the reserved ½ cup of crumbs over the cheesecake.
6. Refrigerate cheesecake for one hour or for up to 48 hours after covering with foil. Before serving, run a metal spatula down the cheesecake's edge to release and remove the pan. Any leftovers should be refrigerated and covered.

63. S'MORES POPS

Prep Time: 10 Mins

Chilling Time: 1 Hr 10 Mins

Total Time: 1 Hr 20 Mins

Serving: 8

Ingredients

- 7 oz marshmallow creme
- 16 graham crackers (halved)
- 16 wooden craft sticks/ sucker sticks
- 2 cups of chocolate chips
- 1 tbsp coconut oil

Instructions

1. Put parchment paper on one cookie sheet.
2. Split the graham crackers in half lengthwise, then arrange half of the crackers onto the baking sheet that has been ready.
3. Drizzle the Graham Crackers in the pan with marshmallow crème. Next, insert the wooden craft stick half way into the marshmallow crème, and cover it with the other half of the graham cracker.
4. Put the pan in the freezer for ten minutes or so.
5. Microwave the chocolate morsels and coconut oil in 30 second increments, stirring intermittently, until the mixture becomes smooth in a medium-sized bowl.
6. Dip the graham cracker sandwiches in the chocolate while holding the popsicle stick. And make sure the graham crackers are fully covered in chocolate by using a spoon.
7. Reposition them on the ready-made cookie sheet. The chocolate will then solidify if you refrigerate the pan.
8. Simply take the pops out of the refrigerator one to two minutes before serving to enjoy them whenever they're ready.

64. OATMEAL S'MORE COOKIES

Prep Time: 20 Mins. + Chilling

Bake Time: 10 Mins/Batch + Cooling

Total Time: 40 Mins

Serving: 5 ½ Dozen

Ingredients

- ½ cup of softened butter
- ½ cup of shortening
- 1 cup of packed brown sugar
- ½ cup of sugar
- 2 large eggs, room temperature
- 1 ½ tsp vanilla extract
- 3 cups of all-purpose flour
- 1 tsp baking soda
- ¼ tsp salt
- 1½ cups of old-fashioned oats
- 1 cup of semisweet chocolate chips
- 1 cup of miniature marshmallows

Directions

1. Combine the butter, shortening, and sugars in a large bowl and beat until light and fluffy, about 5 to 7 minutes. Add eggs one by one, whisk well after each addition. Mix in the vanilla, combine flour, baking soda, and salt; add to creamed mixture gradually and thoroughly combine. After mixing in the marshmallows, chocolate chips, and oats, chill the dough for about 30 minutes.
2. Roll dough tbsp into balls and set on baking sheets that have been buttered two inches apart. Bake for 8-10 minutes at 350°, or until golden brown. Before removing from the pans to cool entirely, let them cool for one or two minutes.

65. STUFFED S'MORES FRENCH TOAST

Total Time: 1 Hr

Serving: 5

Ingredients

- 3 slices of chocolate chip brioche (or plain sliced bread)
- 2 eggs
- 1 tsp vanilla
- 1 splash of milk or half/half
- 1 cup of mini marshmallows
- ¼ cup of mini chocolate chips
- 1 crushed up graham cracker
- 2 tbsp powdered sugar
- 2 tsp brown sugar for sprinkling
- 2 pads of butter for cooking

Instructions

1. Combine the two eggs, milk or half-and-half, and vanilla in a shallow dish. Gently dip into the egg mixture and, to keep it from sticking, place in the pan with a dab of butter. Add some brown sugar to make a very delicious crust. Let it sit for about one minute, then flip it over and put brown sugar on top again. Take off the heat. Cut into a minimum of two slices. Place little chocolate chips and marshmallows in each layer, then stack. If you don't have a means to roast the marshmallows, you may still use the heat to scorch the chocolate chips and marshmallows in each layer without becoming charred. Lastly, sprinkle chocolate chips, marshmallows, and crumbled graham crackers over top. Serve with a dusting of powdered sugar. The dish is already rather sweet, so you really don't need any syrup.
2. Now serve with a dollop of butter and syrup. Enjoy with a little dusting of powdered sugar!

66. GINGERSNAP S'MORES

Prep Time: 15 Mins

Cook Time: 15 Mins

Inactive Time: 10 Mins

Total Time: 40 Mins

Servings: 11

Ingredients

- 1 (4 oz) stick room temperature unsalted butter
- 1 cup of granulated sugar, divided
- ½ cup of lightly packed dark brown sugar
- ⅓ cup of molasses
- 1 large egg
- 1 ½ tsp ground ginger
- 1 tsp ground cinnamon
- ¼ tsp ground cloves
- ½ tsp fine salt
- 1 ½ tsp baking soda
- 2¼ cups of (10.12 ounces) all-purpose flour
- 1 cup of (6 ounces) milk chocolate chips
- Marshmallow fluff

Instructions

1. Set oven temperature to 350°F. Put parchment paper on baking sheets.
2. Whisk the butter, brown sugar, and ½ cup of granulated sugar in a large bowl for two minutes with an electric mixer until they are light and fluffy. Beat in the egg and the molasses after adding them. Add the ginger, cloves, cinnamon, baking soda, salt, and flour, blending them well.
3. Transfer the leftover half cup of sugar into a shallow dish. Before putting the dough on the baking sheet, scoop it into 1 ½ tbsp balls and roll them in sugar. For 13 to 15 minutes, bake.
4. The chocolate chips should be heated in the microwave in 30-second increments while stirring in between each burst, in a heat-safe bowl. Cover half of the cookies with a dollop of chocolate on the middle bottom side. Place a generous amount of marshmallow fluff onto the underside of the lingering cookies. Lightly toast the marshmallow fluff using a cooking flame, taking care not to burn the cookie itself.

Place a chocolate biscuit between two marshmallow cookies. Proceed with the leftover cookies.

5. If using entire marshmallows, toast them with a kitchen torch, over a fire pit, or on a stove burner until they are golden brown. After placing the marshmallow on top of the chocolate, sandwich it between two cookies. Serve immediately.

67. S'MORES MILKSHAKES

Prep Time: 5 Mins

Cook Time: 5 Mins

Total Time: 10 Mins

Servings: 2

Ingredients

- 8-10 jumbo marshmallows
- 3 graham crackers sheets
- 1 Hershey bar
- ½ cup of whole milk
- 2 cups of vanilla ice cream
- 2-3 large marshmallows

Instructions

1. Place marshmallows on a baking sheet coated with paper. To toast to your preference, broil for five to seven minutes on the second-highest rack setting (note: rotate for even toasting). You may add the toasted marshmallows to this step and leave them aside if you wish to decorate your milkshake with them.
2. Finely crush or crumble Graham Crackers into a bag. Transfer to a platter.
3. Melt the chocolate in a small dish for 30 seconds, then for 15 seconds at a time until it is completely melted.
4. Before dipping the rim of your milkshake glasses into the crumbled graham cracker, dip it in the chocolate. If you'd like, use a spoon to sprinkle any extra chocolate inside the glass and leave it aside.
5. Pour the milk, marshmallows, and ice cream into the blender. Process till smooth.
6. Pour into prepared cups, then top with more toasted marshmallows, if desired.

68. S'MORES CRESCENT ROLLS

Prep Time: 15 Mins

Cook Time: 10 Mins

Total Time: 25 Mins

Servings: 8

Ingredients

- 1 can (8 ounces) refrigerated crescent rolls
- ¼ cup of Nutella (chocolate hazelnut spread)
- 1 cup of milk chocolate chips
- 1 cup of mini marshmallows
- 1 rectangle graham cracker, broken in small pieces

Instructions

1. Warm the oven up to 375°F. Use nonstick spray or line a cookie sheet with parchment paper.
2. Take out of the can of crescent rolls. Divide into eight triangles.
3. Place one tsp of Nutella on top of each crescent, followed by eight marshmallows, five chocolate chips, and a few broken graham cracker pieces.
4. Gently roll up into a crescent shape, rolling from the broad end toward the tip.
5. Bake till golden brown, 10 minutes or more. Take out of the oven and pour some additional melted Nutella over the top. Five minutes should pass before serving. Have fun!

69. S'MORES SUGAR COOKIE RECIPE

Prep Time: 15 Mins

Cook Time: 11 Mins

Broil Time: 2 Mins

Total Time: 28 Mins

Servings: 12

Ingredients

- ½ cup of salted butter
- 1 cup of granulated sugar
- 1 large egg
- 1 ½ tsp vanilla extract
- ¼ cup of whole milk
- 2 cups of all-purpose flour
- ½ cup of crushed graham crackers about ½ sleeve
- ½ tsp baking powder
- ¼ tsp baking soda
- 10-12 s'mores style square marshmallows
- 2 Hershey's milk chocolate bars

Instructions

1. Set oven temperature to 375°F.
2. Whisk the butter and sugar in a large mixing bowl on medium-high speed with an electric hand mixer while the oven preheats. If you have a stand mixer, you may also use it. Whisk until smooth, about 2-3 minutes.
3. Pour in the vanilla and the egg. Mix for an extra minute to properly incorporate the egg.
4. Add the flour, graham cracker crumbs, baking powder, and baking soda gradually on low speed until the cookie dough is completely combined and there are no dry pockets left.
5. Drop heaping tbsp-sized dollops of dough onto a baking sheet. After baking for 11 minutes, space the cookies apart by approximately one inch.
6. After all of the cookie dough has baked, place two Hershey chocolate pieces and a marshmallow on top of half of the cookies. Broil the cookies on high for approximately a minute, until the marshmallows are golden brown.

7. Take the pan out of the oven and place the remaining cookies on top of each S'more sandwich.
8. Serve immediately and enjoy!

70. TOASTED S'MORES COOKIES

Prep Time: 10 Mins

Cook Time: 12 Mins

Total Time: 22 Mins

Servings: 18

Ingredients

- ½ cup of softened unsalted butter
- ¾ cup of packed light brown sugar
- 2 tbsp honey (measured accurately - too much will make the cookies spread)
- 1 large egg room temperature
- 1 tsp pure vanilla extract
- 1½ cups of all-purpose flour
- ½ tsp baking soda
- ½ tsp ground cinnamon
- ½ tsp salt
- 1 cup of dark chocolate chips
- 18 big marshmallows (vegan preferred because they don't melt as easily)
- ½ cup of graham crackers crushed into crumbs

Instructions

1. Soft butter and brown sugar should be combined in a large bowl and beaten on medium speed for two minutes (or by hand with a broad spatula or in a stand mixer with a paddle attachment) until smooth, creamy, and slightly fluffy. Mix honey, egg, and vanilla well by beating them in.
2. Mix flour, baking soda, cinnamon, and salt; whisk to incorporate evenly. Mix the flour mixture just until combined after adding it to the creamed butter mixture. Fold the chocolate pieces in until they are distributed uniformly.
3. Refrigerate the bowl for half an hour with a cover on.
4. Turn the oven on to 375°F. Place parchment paper between two big baking sheets.

5. Form the cookie dough into balls by scooping about 2 tbsp at a time. Next, flatten it onto your hand to form a disk. After centering a big marshmallow in the middle of the dough disk, cover the marshmallow with the cookie dough, leaving the top uncovered. After rolling the dough ball in graham cracker crumbs, lay it on the prepared baking sheets, leaving a 2-inch space between each one.

6. Bake for ten to twelve minutes, until the marshmallows are toasted on top and the color is uniformly brown. The marshmallow that spills onto the baking sheets will be quite sticky while still warm, so allow the cookies to cool fully before placing them back on the sheets.

71. SOFT AND CHEWY S'MORE COOKIES

Prep Time: 25 Mins

Cook Time: 8 Mins

Total Time: 33 Mins

Servings: 3

Ingredients

- ¾ cup of softened butter
- ½ cup of granulated sugar
- ½ cup of packed brown sugar
- 1 egg
- 1 tsp vanilla extract
- 1¼ cups of all-purpose flour
- 1¼ cups of graham cracker crumbs
- ¼ tsp salt
- ½ tsp baking soda
- 1½ cups of semi-sweet chocolate chips
- 2 chopped Hershey bars
- 1 cup of mini marshmallows

Instructions

1. Cream sugars and butter together; stir in egg and vanilla.
2. Mix in baking soda, salt, flour, and graham cracker crumbs. Blend until well combined.
3. Add chocolate chunks and chips and stir until thoroughly mixed.

4. Drop onto cookie sheet by heaping tsp, spacing them about 3 inches apart.
5. Now bake for eight minutes at 375 degrees F. Remove the marshmallows and push them firmly into the cookies. Return to oven and continue cooking for 3–4 minutes, until it's done.

72. EASY S'MORES BITES RECIPE

Prep Time: 10 Mins

Cook Time: 10 Mins

Total Time: 20 Mins

Servings: 1

Ingredients

- 7 graham crackers
- ¼ cup of powdered sugar
- 6 tbsp butter
- 2 (1.55 oz) Hershey bars, broken into squares
- 12 marshmallows cut in half

Instructions

1. Preheat oven to 350 degrees. Grind the graham crackers to a fine powder in a food processor or Ziplock bag using a rolling pin. Put the graham crackers, powdered sugar, and butter in a small bowl and mix well. Fill each of the 24 wells of a mini muffin tray with about one tbsp of the mixture; press in the graham cracker crumbs firmly with your fingertips.
2. After that, bake for 4 minutes and remove from oven. One piece of chocolate should be fully inserted into each muffin tin, followed by a half-marshmallow. Place in oven for two more minutes to soften marshmallows.

73. PEANUT BUTTER S'MOREOS

Prep Time: 3 Mins

Cook Time: 2 Mins

Total Time: 5 Mins

Servings: 10

Ingredients

- 20 whole Oreos
- 10 whole marshmallows
- 5 tbsp salted natural creamy peanut butter (slightly warmed till pourable)

Instructions

1. Set the oven rack to the second-highest position and turn the broiler on high.
2. Arrange ten Oreos (modify based on batch size) onto a baking sheet, then cover with a marshmallow (or wait a few minutes).
3. Watch carefully and broil on high for one to three minutes, or until toasted and deeply golden brown.
4. Take out of the oven, then cover each with half a spoonful of peanut butter (warm it up in the microwave for a little while if it's not pourable) and a second Oreo.
5. Consume immediately.

74. S'MORES NO BAKE COOKIES

Total Time: 15 Mins

Servings: 36

Ingredients

- 3 tbsp butter
- 10 ounces mini marshmallows
- 11-12 ounces milk chocolate chips
- 8 cups of (11.7-ounce box) golden grahams cereal

Instructions

1. Put one cup of chocolate chips and one cup of mini marshmallows in a bowl and leave it aside.
2. Put the last few marshmallows in a bowl that can go in the microwave. Add the butter and give it a 30-second microwave. Try to agitate the blend. Then continue to microwave in 30-second intervals until the mixture can be stirred. Pour in the remaining chocolate chips and stir to melt them, when the marshmallow-butter mixture is smooth (if the mixture is "close," use a 15-second burst).
3. Stir to coat after adding the cereal.
4. Add the chips and marshmallows you set out. Stir until evenly distributed.
5. Now drop onto baking sheets lined with wax paper by rounded tsp. Mixture will solidify as it cools.

75. COOKOUT CARAMEL S'MORES

Total Time: 10 Mins

Servings: 4

Ingredients

- 8 large marshmallows
- 2 tsp fat-free chocolate syrup
- 8 low-fat graham crackers (2 ½-inch square)
- 2 tsp fat-free caramel topping

Directions

1. Toast marshmallows 6 inches from medium-hot flame with a long-handled fork until golden brown, flipping them from time to time.
2. Pour chocolate syrup onto four graham crackers and place two toasted marshmallows on top of each. Add a caramel topping drizzle. Place the remaining Graham Crackers on top.

76. RAINBOW S'MOREO COOKIES

Prep Time: 15 Mins. + Chilling

Bake Time: 10 Mins/Batch + Freezing

Cook Time: 25 Mins

Servings: 2 Dozen

Ingredients

- ½ cup of softened unsalted butter
- 1 cup of sugar
- 1 large egg
- 1 tsp vanilla extract
- ½ cup of baking cocoa
- ¾ cup of graham cracker crumbs
- ¾ cup of all-purpose flour
- 1 tsp baking powder
- ¼ tsp kosher salt
- 1 jar (7 ounces) marshmallow creme
- Rainbow sprinkles

Directions

1. Preheat your oven to 350 degrees. Whisk butter and sugar for 5-7 minutes until frothy. Add vanilla and egg, and beat. Stir in chocolate. Mix the flour, baking powder, salt, and cracker crumbs in a separate bowl and then gently fold them into the creamed mixture. Put in the fridge for at least 30 minutes, until it's firm.
2. Roll dough into 1-inch spheres. Place on baking pans lined with paper, 2 inches apart. Press down using the sugar-coated base of a glass. Bake 6 to 8 minutes, until it's set. Cool on the pans for three minutes. Transfer to wire racks so they can cool fully.
3. Coat the bottoms of half of the cookies with marshmallow creme, then top with the remaining cookies. Sprinkle sprinkles over the borders. Serve right away or freeze the cookies in freezer-safe containers, being sure to use wax paper between layers. Before serving, quickly defrost the cookies.

77. S'MORES CHOCOLATE TART

Prep Time: 45 Mins

Chilling Time: 4 Hr

Total Time: 4 Hrs 45 Mins

Servings: 12

Ingredients

For the biscuit base

- 275 g digestive biscuits crushed into crumbs
- 135 g butter or baking spread melted

For the filling

- 125 g marshmallow fluff, optional

For the chocolate ganache

- 275 ml double cream
- 275 g dark chocolate
- A pinch of salt

For the topping & decoration

- 100 ml double cream
- ¼ tsp vanilla extract
- 1 tsp icing sugar
- 65 g marshmallows
- ½ tbsp cocoa powder

Instructions

1. First, crush the biscuits into crumbs using a food processor or a dish or freezer bag. Be cautious not to overwork them.
2. Fill a bowl with the biscuit crumbs. Melt the butter and stir it in.
3. Fill a 9-inch loose-bottomed tart tin with the biscuit mixture, pressing it into the sides and bottom. To press it uniformly around the base and edges, you can use a shot glass or an American cup measure.
4. Place the biscuit foundation in the refrigerator for half an hour.
5. Scatter the marshmallow fluff over the tart's bottom.

6. Heat the double cream in a skillet over low heat, stirring often, to produce the chocolate ganache.
7. Remove the cream from the heat when it begins to steam. Add the chocolate to the cream and wait for a few minutes before stirring until everything melts together. Add the pinch of salt and stir.
8. Spoon the ganache over the marshmallow powder in the pastry base. Spread it out gently, then use a little pallet knife to smooth the top. To smooth out the ganache and get rid of any air bubbles, you may also very lightly tap the tin on the surface.
9. Place in the refrigerator to set for at least 4 hours, or better yet, overnight.
10. After removing the pie from the tin, sprinkle the tart's top with cocoa powder using a fine sieve.
11. Beat together the double cream, vanilla extract, and icing sugar, then pipe the mixture around the tart's edges.
12. Place the marshmallows on a platter and toast them with a kitchen blowtorch. Or you may briefly place them under the grill.
13. Top the whipped cream with the toasted marshmallows.
14. Serve immediately. Keep leftovers refrigerated and consume them within three days.

78. FUDGY S'MORES BROWNIES

Prep Time: 15 Mins

Bake Time: 25 Mins + Cooling

Total Time: 40 Mins

Servings: 1 Dozen

Ingredients

- 1⅓ cups of softened butter
- 2 ⅔ cups of sugar
- 4 large eggs, room temperature
- 1 tbsp vanilla extract
- 2 cups of all-purpose flour
- 1 cup of baking cocoa
- ½ tsp salt
- 1 cup of coarsely crushed Golden Grahams
- 1¾ cups of miniature marshmallows

- 4 ounces chopped milk chocolate

Directions

1. Turn the oven on to 350°. Then, cream butter & sugar in a large bowl for five to seven minutes, until it's light and fluffy. Add vanilla and eggs and beat. Next, mix flour, cocoa, and salt in a bowl and gradually beat into the creamed mixture.
2. After that, grease a 13 x 9-inch baking pan with oil. Don't overbake; bake for 25 to 30 minutes, until a skewer inserted into the middle pulls out with moist crumbs.
3. Warm up the broiler. Top prepared brownies with cereal and marshmallows; broil 5-6 inches from the heat source for 30 to 45 seconds, until the marshmallows turn golden brown. Sprinkle with chopped chocolate immediately. Wrap the chocolate in foil and let it there for approximately five minutes, until it starts to melt. Remove foil and let cool entirely in the pan on a wire rack. Cut into bars.

79. S'MORES CHOCOLATE POTS

Total Time: 35 Mins

Servings: 6

Ingredients

- 4 digestive biscuits
- 120g salted caramel sauce
- 200ml double cream
- 150g of 70% dark chocolate, divided into little bits
- 2 eggs, separated
- 120g caster sugar
- ⅛ tsp cream of tartar

Directions

1. Place the biscuits in a bowl and pound them into a fine crumble with a rolling pin. Spoon the salted caramel sauce over the divided portions into each of the six tiny serving glasses.
2. In a mixing bowl set over a pan of moderately simmering water, melt the chocolate with a dash of salt. After melting, take out of the pan and allow to cool.
3. Whip the cream to soft peaks with electric beaters.

4. Smoothly whisk the chocolate mixture after adding the egg yolks. Beat in ¼ of the cream after adding it. Add the remaining cream and combine by folding. To firm up, divide amongst the glasses and refrigerate for 30 minutes. Take out of the refrigerator and let it to room temperature before serving.

5. After that, whisk egg whites, sugar, and cream of tartar in a heatproof mixing bowl using electric beaters once the pots have set. Place over a pan of moderately simmering water and whisk constantly for 6-8 minutes, until the egg whites have quadrupled in volume and become glossy and brilliant. After taking the mixture off the heat, whisk it for another four to five minutes, or until soft peaks form.

6. After gently blow-torching the marshmallow tops until brown, spoon the marshmallow over the chocolate pots (if the glasses are heatproof, you can alternatively do this on a grill). Serve immediately.

(SIMPLE RECIPES)

80. S'MORES POT DE CRÈME

Prep Time: 10 Mins

Cook Time: 50 Mins

Cool Time: 1 Hr

Total Time: 2 Hr

Servings: 2

Ingredients

Pot de Creme

- ¾ cup of whipping cream
- 2 tbsp milk
- 3 ounces dark or bittersweet chocolate
- 3 egg yolks
- 1 to 2 tbsp sugar

S'mores Topping

- 1 oz dark or semisweet chocolate
- 2 handfuls mini marshmallows (¾ to 1 cup)

- 4 squares graham crackers

Instructions

1. Set oven temperature to 325°F.
2. Take two 8 oz (1 cup) ramekins and place them in a baking dish, such as a 9 x 9-inch square pan, or any baking dish big enough to hold both (if using smaller ramekins, see note). Fill the baking dish with water until the ramekins' sides are almost halfway up.
3. Remove two medium-sized to large-sized mixing bowls, one of which must be microwave-safe. Fill the bowl suitable for the microwave with the cream and milk. Heat in microwave for 30-second intervals until the milk and cream combination is extremely hot but not yet boiling. This requires two to three minutes.
4. Add chocolate, broken up into small bits, to the heated cream and milk mixture.
5. Whisk the chocolate and the cream milk mixture together until they are well blended. It ought to resemble hot cocoa. Set aside.
6. Transfer the sugar and egg yolks to the other bowl. You may use the same whisk you used in the previous step; there's no need to wash it first. Whisk them together until well blended.
7. As you slowly add the heated chocolate and cream mixture to the egg yolks, whisk well. After that, fill the ramekins with the chocolate mixture. Once they become slightly jiggly and no longer liquidy, bake for 35 to 45 minutes.
8. Take out of the oven and let cool for around sixty minutes. If serving later, place plastic wrap over the ramekins and place them in the refrigerator.
9. When ready to serve, put the chocolate in a small bowl that is safe to be placed in the microwave and melt it in 15-second intervals, stirring after each one. Set aside.
10. Set the broiler on "High" in the oven. Crush two squares of graham cracker and add them to the top of the chocolate mixture in the ramekins. Sprinkle some mini marshmallows over the graham crackers. Place in the oven and toast the marshmallows for 60 to 120 seconds, monitoring them often, until they reach your desired toasty ness.
11. Transfer the liquefied chocolate onto the marshmallows and scatter the leftover graham crackers on top. Serve warm.

81. S'MORES CAMPFIRE CONES

Prep Time: 10 Mins

Cook Time: 15 Mins

Total Time: 25 Mins

Servings: 6

Ingredients

- 1 (1.5 oz) bar milk chocolate candy bar
- 6 sugar cones
- ¾ cup of mini marshmallows
- 6 sheets aluminum foil

Directions

1. Make a campfire and let it burn until coals form a bed on top of it. Rake the coals into a level bed on one side of the fire.
2. Cut chocolate bar into twelve equal halves.
3. Put two tbsp of marshmallows and two pieces of chocolate into each cone.
4. Wrap each filled cone in foil and lay it over the bonfire, indirectly over the flame. Cook until gooey and melted, about 5 minutes, turning halfway through.

82. GOLDEN GRAHAMS S'MORES BARS

Prep Time: 5 Mins

Total Time: 30 Mins

Servings: 12

Ingredients

- ⅓ cup of unsalted butter
- pinch of salt
- 16-ounce bag of marshmallows
- 5 ½ cups of Golden Grahams
- ½ cup of milk chocolate
- 1½ cups of mini marshmallows (for folding into the bars)

Instructions

1. Spray cooking spray on a 9 × 9 pan and put it aside.
2. Melt the butter in a large pot over a medium heat.
3. Using a rubber spatula, whisk in the normal marshmallows and salt, scraping down the edges to ensure the marshmallows don't burn. Remove the marshmallows from the heat source as soon as they have melted.
4. Combine the marshmallow mixture and Golden Grahams cereal in a large bowl. Fold ingredients together using a rubber spatula.
5. Add the small marshmallows and chocolate and stir.
6. Press down to make a uniform layer as you spoon ingredients into the pan that has been prepared.
7. Put in the refrigerator for at least 20 minutes to let it set. After they're firm, cut the S'mores bars into 12 rectangles using a sharp knife. Enjoy!

83. MICROWAVE S'MORES

Prep Time: 3 Mins

Cook Time: 1 Min

Total Time: 4 Mins

Servings: 4

Ingredients

- 4 large marshmallows
- 4 full graham crackers
- 2 oz chocolate

Instructions

1. Spoon the graham cracker halves onto a platter that is safe to use in the microwave. Fill each half with a few marshmallows and chocolate. Alternatively, leave the chocolate off for now if you don't want it to melt.
2. After that, microwave them on high for 20-30 seconds until the marshmallows swell to about twice their original size.
3. Then take the plate off and top the entire S'more with the other half of the graham cracker. Or add the chocolate if you didn't want it to melt. Enjoy!

84. CHOCOLATE DIPPED PEANUT BUTTER S'MORES

Prep Time: 20 Mins

Total Time: 50 Mins

Servings: 8

Ingredients

- ½ cup of smooth peanut butter
- 16 graham cracker squares (halved)
- ½ cup of chocolate-hazelnut spread
- 8 marshmallows
- 1 package white almond bark
- 1 package milk chocolate chips

Decorating suggestions

- chopped pistachios
- chopped pretzels
- rainbow sprinkles and chocolate sprinkles

Instructions

1. Spread a big dollop of peanut butter on one side of 8 cracker squares, followed by the chocolate-hazelnut spread over the remaining 8 pieces.
2. Place the marshmallows on two metal skewers and gently roast them over a stovetop heat. Top each of the graham crackers coated in peanut butter with a single roasted marshmallow. Place the chocolate-covered crackers on top, then carefully sandwich.
3. Heat separate glass dishes with boiling water to melt the milk chocolate and white almond bark. Keep the chocolate melted by swirling occasionally while it cools.
4. One by one, dunk half of the sandwiches in the white chocolate, letting any extra drop off, once the toppings are room temperature. Work fast, and then top with any desired sprinkles or toppers. Continue by dipping the remaining four sandwiches in the milk chocolate and then top them with the preferred garnishes.
5. Put in the refrigerator for a minimum of half an hour. After that, you can keep the s'mores in the refrigerator or at room temperature until you're ready to serve!

85. NO-BAKE S'MORES TREATS

Prep Time: 10 Mins

Cook Time: 10 Mins

Total Time: 20 Mins

Servings: 18

Ingredients

- ¼ cup of cubed butter
- 1 package (10 oz) miniature or large marshmallows
- 1 package (12 oz) Golden Grahams (about 8 cups)
- ⅓ cup of melted milk chocolate chips

Instructions

1. Dissolve butter in a large pot over a low heat. Stir in marshmallows (save a few for the top); heat until well combined. Take off the heat. Add cereal and stir until evenly covered.
2. Press into a 13 x 9-inch pan that has been oiled firmly with a buttered spatula. Microwave chocolate for 30 second bursts, swirling occasionally, until it melts. Drizzle bars with melted chocolate chips using a fork. Let cool fully. Divided into bars. Keep in a sealed container.

86. S'MORES CAKE

Prep Time: 1 Hr 35 Mins

Cook Time: 1 Hr 10 Mins

Total Time: 2 Hrs 45 Mins

Servings: 10

Ingredients

For the ganache

- ½ cup of heavy cream
- 4 ounces finely chopped semisweet chocolate
- Pinch of salt
- ½ tsp vanilla extract

For the filling

- 8 crushed whole graham crackers
- 2 tbsp melted unsalted butter
- Pinch of salt
- Vegetable oil, for the spatula
- 1 (16-ounce) container marshmallow cream

For the cake

- Basic chocolate cake, baked and cooled

Basic Chocolate Cake

- Cooking spray
- 1 cup of unsweetened cocoa powder
- 2½ cups of all-purpose flour
- 2 cups of sugar
- 1 ½ tsp baking powder
- 1 tsp baking soda
- 1 tsp salt
- 3 large eggs, at room temperature
- ¾ cup of vegetable oil
- ½ cup of sour cream
- 2 tsp vanilla extract

Directions

1. **Make the ganache:** Heat the heavy cream, chocolate, and salt in a heatproof bowl positioned over a pot of boiling water (do not allow the bowl touch the water), stirring regularly, till the chocolate has melted and ganache is smooth. Add the vanilla and stir. After taking the bowl out of the pan, wait one hour or so, until the ganache is cold and thick but still pourable.

2. **Meanwhile, make the filling:** Set the oven's temperature to 350°F. Combine graham cracker crumbs, melted butter, and salt in a bowl. Organize evenly on a baking sheet. Bake for 8 to 10 minutes, stirring periodically, until toasted; then, allow to cool. When the cake is almost ready to be served, assemble it: Cutting each cake layer in half lengthwise with a long-serrated knife requires caution. Put one half of the cake on a dish. Spread one-third of the marshmallow cream over top using a spoon or lightly oiled offset spatula, stopping approximately 1 inch from the edge (if the marshmallow cream is hard to spread, microwave it for 10-15 seconds to soften it). Over the marshmallow cream, scatter a third of the graham cracker mixture. Continue to create 4 layers, finishing with the cake; set aside a couple of tbsp for the topping made of graham cracker mixture. Drizzle the cake with the ganache, allowing it to run over the sides. Apply the saved graham cracker mixture over top. Serve immediately.

Basic Chocolate Cake

3. Set the oven's temperature to 350°F. Spray two 9-inch round cake pans and cover the bottoms with parchment paper.

4. Combine the cocoa powder with 1½ cups of hot water in a medium bowl and mix until combined; put aside. Combine sugar, flour, baking soda, baking powder, and salt in a big bowl and mix with a whisk. Mix in the eggs, sour cream, vegetable oil, and vanilla. Whip on medium speed for one minute, or until smooth. Lower the speed of the mixer to low and use a rubber spatula to stir the cocoa mixture in a steady stream until it is just incorporated. (There will be little batter.)

5. Divide batter into the prepared pans and tap them against the counter to help it settle. Then bake for 30 to 40 minutes, till a skewer inserted in the middle pulls out clean. After transferring to the racks and cooling for ten minutes, flip the cakes over to cool fully by running a knife over the pan's edge. Take out the parchment. If desired, level the cakes' tops by trimming them with a long-serrated knife.

87. S'MORES DIPPED STRAWBERRIES

Total Time: 20 Mins

Servings: 2

Ingredients

- 8-10 large washed and dried fresh strawberries
- 3 cups of miniature marshmallows
- 1½ cups of dark chocolate melting wafers
- ½ cup of graham cracker crumbs

Instructions

1. Put parchment paper on the rim of a baking sheet. Spray cooking spray on parchment paper and put it aside.
2. To a medium microwaveable bowl, add the small marshmallows. Microwave on HIGH for 30 seconds. Marshmallows will seem puffy. Stir until oozy and melted. Working rapidly, dip each strawberry into the marshmallow goo mixture to about ¾ of its full length. Work quickly since the marshmallow goop mixture solidifies quickly! If necessary, warm the marshmallow mixture in the microwave for an additional five seconds. After dipping the strawberries in the marshmallow mixture, let them sit in the fridge for approximately ten minutes to solidify.
3. Once the layer of marshmallow has hardened, melt the chocolate candy coating in accordance with the instructions on the package, until it is completely smooth. Take each strawberry and dip it approximately two thirds the way into the dark chocolate, letting the excess drop out. Transfer back to the baking sheet and promptly top with a heaping tbsp of graham cracker crumbs. Before serving, let the strawberries' chocolate set. Serve immediately.

88. S'MORES NACHOS

Total Time: 5 Mins

Servings: 4

Ingredients

- 8 rectangular graham crackers
- ¾ cup of milk chocolate chips
- 1½ cups of miniature marshmallows

Instructions

1. Cut every Graham Cracker into four pieces. Place slices in a pie pan without oil. AVOID USING GLASS. Add marshmallows and chocolate chips on top.
2. Broil marshmallows 6 inches from the flame for 30 to 60 seconds, until they are puffed and golden, keeping an eye out for burning.

89. NO BAKE S'MORES CHEESECAKE

Prep Time: 15 Mins

Cook Time: 10 Mins

Setting Time: 6 Hr

Total Time: 6 Hrs 25 Mins

Servings: 12

Ingredients

Base

- 300 g biscuits
- 150 g melted unsalted butter

Cheesecake Filling

- 500 g full fat mascarpone cream cheese
- 100 g icing sugar
- 1 tsp vanilla extract
- 1 x 214g marshmallow fluff tub
- 300 ml double cream

Decoration

- 150 ml double cream
- 2 tbsp icing sugar
- Mini marshmallows
- Biscuit crumbs
- Melted chocolate

Instructions

1. Combine the melted unsalted butter with the digestive biscuits, crushing them with a rolling pin or blitzing them in a food processor.
2. Press into an 8"/20cm deep springform tin; store in the refrigerator.
3. Using an electric mixer (I use my KitchenAid with the whisk attachment), combine the mascarpone cream cheese, vanilla extract, and icing sugar. Whisk until creamy and well blended.
4. Mix in the marshmallow fluff and whisk once more; it will appear lumpy at first, but with persistence, it will become smooth.
5. When the double cream is liquid, add it and whisk until stiff. When the mixture is extremely thick and holds itself when you pull the whisk out, be careful to scrape down the bowl's sides and keep whisking!
6. Smooth over the top layer of the biscuit foundation and chill for at least 6 hours, or better yet, overnight (12+ hours), to let it to set thoroughly.
7. Use a blowtorch to cook some little marshmallows to decorate your s'mores cheesecake so they all stick together beautifully.
8. Crush more biscuits, scatter them evenly, and then pour molten chocolate or chocolate curls over top!
9. ENJOY!

90. NO CHURN S'MORES ICE CREAM

Prep Time: 30 Mins

Chill Time: 6 Hr

Total Time: 6 Hrs 30 Mins

Servings: 6

Ingredients

Graham Crumbles

- ¾ cup of graham cracker crumbs
- 3 tbsp melted butter
- Pinch of salt

S'mores Ice Cream

- 1 (14-oz) can sweeten condensed milk
- 3 tbsp unsweetened cocoa powder
- 2 oz chocolate melted and cooled
- 1 tsp vanilla extract
- 1-pint heavy cream
- 1 container marshmallow fluff

Instructions

To make the graham crumbles

1. Set a baking sheet covered with parchment paper and preheat the oven to 350°F.
2. Combine graham crumbs, butter, and salt until evenly covered. Crumble the ingredients using a fork or with your hands.
3. Next, spread on prepared baking sheet and bake for 8 minutes. Let crumbles cool fully.

To make the ice cream

4. Mix the melted chocolate, vanilla, cocoa powder, and sweetened condensed milk in a medium-sized bowl.
5. Whisk heavy cream on high speed in a large bowl until firm peaks form. Beat in the condensed milk mixture that has been sweetened. Continue whisking until firm peaks form.
6. Spoon about ¼ of the chocolate mixture into a 9" x 5" loaf pan, then top with marshmallow fluff. (To simplify drizzle, you might want to spoon some marshmallow fluff into a dish and microwave it for 5 to 8 seconds.)
7. Lightly toast the marshmallow fluff using a cooking flame. Toasting the marshmallow is unnecessary, and the ice cream still tastes great without it!
8. Over the marshmallow, scatter roughly ⅓ of the graham cracker crumbs. Layers should be repeated twice more, with a final coating of chocolate mixture on top.
9. Place a plastic wrap over it and freeze for at least six hours or overnight.

91. S'MORES MOUSSE PARFAITS

Total Time: 10 Mins

Servings: 4

Ingredients

For Easy Chocolate Mousse

- 1 cup of chocolate chips - using a better-quality chip makes a big difference
- 1 cup of whipping cream
- 1 tsp vanilla extract

For the Parfaits

- 1 cup of graham cracker crumbs
- 1 cup of mini marshmallows
- ½ cup of chocolate mousse prepared
- marshmallows for garnish
- Mini chocolate chips for garnish
- graham cracker crumbs for garnish

Instructions

For the Easy Chocolate Mousse

1. Put the chocolate chips in a bowl made of glass. Dissolve them in the microwave for 30 seconds at 50% power. Stir. Continue until all of the chips have melted. Stir for 30 seconds at 50% power. Let cool for five minutes.
2. Whisk the whipping cream on high speed in a large bowl until soft peaks form. Mix in the vanilla extract.
3. Once the chocolate has melted, add it and whip until it is combined.

To assemble parfaits

4. Put the cups or plates you intend to use in a line.
5. Start by filling each glass's bottom with a spoonful or pipette of chocolate mousse.
6. Next, fill each glass with a layer of little marshmallows.
7. Add more chocolate mousse on top.
8. Sprinkle some graham cracker crumbs on top.
9. Serve immediately. Or refrigerate to serve later.

92. S'MORES BROWNIE TRIFLE

Prep Time: 15 Mins

Total Time: 1 Hr 30 Mins

Servings: 12

Ingredients

- 1 box Fudge Brownie Mix
- Water, vegetable oil and eggs for on brownie mix box
- 1 container (8 oz) Cool Whip frozen whipped topping, thawed
- ½ cup of marshmallow creme
- 12 graham crackers
- 2 tbsp chocolate-flavor syrup

Instructions

1. Preheat the oven to 350°F. Cover a 13 by 9-inch pan with foil, leaving some overhanging the pan's sides. Grease the foil's sides and bottom with cooking spray or shortening. As instructed on the package, prepare and bake the brownies. Give the cooling rack about an hour to cool fully.
2. Meanwhile, thoroughly combine marshmallow creme and whipped topping in a medium-sized bowl. Add six graham crackers crumbles to the marshmallow mixture and mix well. Refrigerate after covering.
3. Peel off the foil after using it to lift the brownies out of the pan. Cut brownies into 1-inch pieces. Fill the bottom of a 3-quart trifle dish with half of the brownie pieces. Crumble two graham crackers over the brownies. Place half of the marshmallow mixture on top.
4. Continue layering, and then top with marshmallow mixture. Top with the remaining two Graham Crackers crumbled and cover with chocolate syrup. Serve right away. Keep covered in the fridge.

93. S'MORES MOLTEN LAVA CAKES

Prep Time: 20 Mins

Cook Time: 10 Mins

Total Time: 30 Mins

Servings: 12

Ingredients

Graham Cracker Crust

- 9 finely ground graham cracker sheets (1¼ cups of crumbs)
- 5 tbsp unsalted butter
- ¼ cup of granulated sugar

Molten Lava Cakes

- 4 oz. roughly chopped semi-sweet baking chocolate
- ½ cup of unsalted butter
- 2 whole eggs
- 1 cup of powdered sugar
- 2 egg yolks
- 6 tbsp flour

Marshmallow Topping

- 6 large marshmallows with the equator sliced in half

Instructions

Graham Cracker Crust

1. Set oven temperature to 350°F.
2. Use cupcake liners to line a standard-sized muffin tin. Apply nonstick cooking spray to the liners. Put aside.
3. Put all the ingredients for the Crust into a big bowl. Blend until well blended. Divide the crumbs evenly among the cupcake liners, about 2 ½ tsp for each liner.
4. Crumble crumbs into the bottom and ¾ up the edges of each liner using a tbsp. They don't have to be flawless or even.

Molten Lava Cakes

5. Put the butter and baking chocolate in a big bowl that is safe to microwave for one minute, until the butter melts. Then, whisk the mixture until it's smooth. Add sugar and stir until creamy. Add the eggs and egg yolks, and use a hand whisk to beat for one minute. Just enough flour should be folded in.
6. Spoon mixture evenly into prepared crusts. If there is batter over the graham crackers, that's acceptable. Bake for nine to eleven minutes, until the centers are still mushy but the sides are firm (not jiggly).

Marshmallow Topping

7. Remove from the oven and top each pie with half a marshmallow. Broil 6" apart from the broiler for one to two minutes, till it's brown.
8. Remove pies with cupcake liners after letting them cool for a minute. Serve immediately for a molten center, since the pie will continue to cook as it cools. They will still be tasty with a gooey middle if you can't serve them right away. They just won't be as runny and molten-like.

94. S'MORES PUDDING PARFAIT

Prep Time: 10 Mins

Inactive: 5 Mins

Total Time: 15 Mins

Servings: 4

Ingredients

- 3 cups of milk
- 1 (5.9-ounce) box chocolate instant pudding
- 10 graham crackers
- 2 cups of mini marshmallows

Instructions

1. Prepare four parfait or wine vinegar glasses. Place the milk in the freezer for 20 minutes before starting to prepare the pudding.
2. Mix pudding mix and milk in a medium-sized bowl until thoroughly mixed and slightly thickened. Give it five minutes.

3. Place Graham Crackers in a zipped plastic bag, and use a rolling pin to cut them into small bits. Place around a quarter cup or so of the pudding at the base of every glass. After the graham crackers have been smashed, sprinkle over a layer of marshmallows. Layer each component again, completing the mixture with the marshmallows. Light a kitchen torch and gently brown the top layer of marshmallows. Serve.

95. S'MORES BUNDT CAKE

Prep Time: 40 Mins

Cook Time: 50 Mins

Cool Time: 2 Hr

Total Time: 3 Hrs 30 Mins

Servings: 1

Ingredients

- 1½ cups of room-temperature softened unsalted butter
- 2 ⅔ cups of granulated sugar
- 6 large eggs, at room temperature
- 2 ¼ cups of sifted cake flour
- ⅔ cup of finely ground graham cracker crumbs
- 1 ½ tsp kosher salt
- ½ tsp baking soda
- 1 cup of whole buttermilk at room temperature
- 2 tbsp pure vanilla extract
- ¼ cup of black cocoa powder
- ½ tsp espresso powder

Milk Chocolate Ganache

- 6 ounces chopped milk chocolate bars
- ⅓ cup of heavy whipping cream

Toppings

- Large marshmallows

Garnish

- broken milk chocolate bars
- roughly crushed graham crackers

Instructions

1. Set the oven to 325°F. Brush baking spray on a 12-cup Bundt pan. While you are making the batter, freeze the pan for about twenty minutes.
2. Mix the sugar and butter in a stand mixer bowl using the paddle attachment. Whip on medium speed for about five or six minutes, until the mixture is light and fluffy.
3. Gently whisk in each egg as you add it, one at a time. Scrape the bowl as required.
4. Mix the flour, baking soda, salt, and graham cracker crumbs in another medium-sized bowl. Whisk the vanilla essence and buttermilk together in a separate small dish.
5. Turn the mixer down to low. Mix flour mixture and buttermilk alternately, starting and finishing with flour.
6. Pour roughly 4 cups of the batter into the medium bowl. Stir in the espresso and chocolate powders. Mix well by folding in.
7. Place 1 cup of the black batter in a large piping bag. Slice off the piping bag's tip. Transfer one cup of the basic batter into an additional large piping bag. Slice off the piping bag's tip. Alternately, pipe batters straight into the grooves in the prepared pan, filling them to a ¾ inch from the top of the central tube to the outside rim. Carefully distribute batter into the grooves and up the pan's sides using an offset spatula. To seal any spaces between the batter, alternate between piping and spreading additional batter into each groove.
8. Once there is no more batter, fill the piping bags again and continue the procedure. Remove any air bubbles and spread the batter into the grooves by tapping the pan on the counter.
9. Bake for 45 to 50 minutes, until a cake tester inserted into the center pulls out clean. Then cool cake in the pan for 10 minutes. Then, loosen the sides and take the cake out of the pan. Transfer cake to cooling rack to complete cooling.
10. Heat heavy cream in a microwave-safe bowl to produce ganache. Toss the chopped chocolate in a medium bowl with the heated heavy cream. After letting it settle for one or two minutes, stir until smooth. Apply right away.

11. Transfer to a cake dish for serving. Pour milk chocolate ganache into a large piping bag with a large round tip. Put the ganache into the cake's cooled grooves using a pastry bag. Arrange the huge marshmallows in the center. Lightly roast the marshmallows using a cooking torch. Add chocolate and graham cracker pieces as cake garnishes.

96. PEANUT BUTTER S'MORES BARS

Prep Time: 10 Mins

Cook Time: 25 Mins

Additional Time: 2 Hr

Total Time: 2 Hrs 35 Mins

Servings: 24

Ingredients

- 2 cups of creamy peanut butter not natural
- 2 eggs
- 2 cups of granulated sugar
- 8 ounces marshmallow creme
- 4 (1.5-ounce) milk chocolate bars

Instructions

1. First, combine peanut butter, eggs, and sugar in a medium mixing bowl. Split the dough in half, then transfer one half into an 11 x 7-inch baking pan that has been buttered.
2. Place the chocolate bars on top of the peanut butter dough after spreading the marshmallow crème over it.
3. Top with the remaining half of the peanut butter dough, and bake for 22 to 24 minutes at 350 degrees, until it's firm and gently browned around the edges.
4. Now remove from oven and cool for 30 minutes. Put in the fridge to cool for a couple of hours. (This will help the chocolate set once again; otherwise, it would be mushy). Slice into bars and present.

97. S'MORES FUDGE

Prep Time: 10 Mins

Cook Time: 10 Mins

Additional Time: 3 Hrs

Total Time: 3 Hrs 20 Mins

Servings: 30

Ingredients

- 8 honey graham crackers, crushed and divided
- 1-pound semisweet chocolate chips
- 1 (14 ounce) can sweetened condensed milk
- ¼ cup of unsalted butter
- 2 tbsp vanilla extract
- 1 (10.5 ounce) package miniature marshmallows

Directions

1. Peel and stick parchment paper into an 11 x 7-inch baking pan. Place half of the crumbled graham crackers into the dish's bottom. Put aside.
2. Melt the butter, chocolate chips, condensed milk, and vanilla in the top of a double boiler over boiling water. next, scrape down the edges with a rubber spatula and stir the mixture often to avoid scorching.
3. Fill the baking dish halfway with the melted chocolate mixture, then top with half of the marshmallows. Continue layering the chocolate mixture, marshmallows, and broken graham crackers.
4. Place in the fridge and let it cool for three to five hours or overnight.

98. S'MORES MACARONS

Prep Time: 30 Mins

Cook Time: 20 Mins

Resting Time: 40 Mins

Total Time: 1 Hr 30 Mins

Servings: 20

Ingredients

Macaron

- 200 grams powdered sugar
- 65 grams almond flour
- 45 grams graham crackers
- 90 grams egg whites
- 30 grams granulated sugar

Marshmallow Buttercream

- ½ cup of unsalted butter softened at room temperature
- 1 cup of marshmallow fluff homemade or store-bought
- 2 cups of powdered sugar
- 2 tbsp milk

Milk Chocolate Ganache

- ½ cup of heavy cream
- 6 ounces milk chocolate chips

Instructions

To make the Macarons

1. Place the graham crackers, almond flour, and powdered sugar in a food processor. Process till everything is perfect.
2. After that, whisk egg whites with a handheld mixer until they get thicker. Add granulated sugar and whisk until firm peaks form.
3. Take care not to overmix as you gently fold the beaten egg whites into the crushed almond and graham cracker mixture until just incorporated. It should be 40-65 folds of "molten lava" but not runny.

4. Spoon batter into a piping bag that has a round tip measuring 0.4 inches (10 millimeters).
5. Pipe 1 ½ inch (4 centimeter) rounds at least 2 inches (5 centimeters) apart onto a baking sheet covered with parchment paper. Continue with the other baking sheets.
6. Remove any extra bubbles by tapping the baking sheets firmly on the counter. Allow it rest, uncovered, for 30-40 minutes to form a shell.
7. Turn the oven on to 300°F, or 150°C.
8. To firm up the macaron tops, bake for 15–20 minutes. Cool on the baking pan before removing.

To make the Milk Chocolate Ganache

9. Heat a small saucepan with the cream over medium heat. Take off from the heat just before it boils and stir in the chocolate chunks. After letting it sit for 30 seconds, blend until it's smooth.
10. Place into a small bowl, cover, and chill, stirring periodically, until solid enough to pipe.

To make the Marshmallow Buttercream

11. Whisk the butter and marshmallow fluff together until smooth in a large bowl.
12. Beat in the powdered sugar gradually. Add enough milk, beating until a light and creamy marshmallow buttercream is achieved. Store in the fridge until required.

To assemble

13. Based on the forms that most closely match, pair the cooled macaron shells.
14. Pipe a little dollop of chocolate ganache and a second dollop of marshmallow buttercream onto the bottom of each shell.
15. Cover gently with the second macaron shell's bottom. Press together gently until the chocolate is all the way to the edges. Continue with the remaining duos.
16. Store in the fridge in single layers for up to one week or 24 hours. Before serving, let it come to room temperature for one hour.

99. S'MORES CUPCAKES

Prep Time: 45 Mins

Cook Time: 20 Mins

Total Time: 1 Hr 5 Mins

Servings: 36

Ingredients

For the graham cracker bottom

- 3 cups of crushed graham crackers (about 2 packages)
- ⅔ cup of unsalted melted butter
- ½ cup of granulated sugar

For the cupcakes

- 2 cups of granulated white sugar
- 1¾ cups of all-purpose flour
- ¾ cup of natural unsweetened cocoa powder
- 1 ½ tsp baking powder
- 1 ½ tsp baking soda
- 1 tsp kosher salt
- 2 large eggs room temperature
- 1 cup of whole milk
- ½ cup of vegetable oil
- 2 tsp vanilla extract
- 1 cup of boiling water

For the frosting

- 8 large egg whites room temperature
- 2 cups of granulated sugar
- ½ tsp cream of tartar
- 2 tsp vanilla extract
- 36 Hershey chocolate squares

Instructions

Make the graham cracker bottom

1. Set the oven's temperature to 350. Put cupcake liners in two regular muffin pans and set them aside.
2. Add sugar, melted butter, and graham cracker crumbs; whisk until thoroughly incorporated.
3. Put 1 spoonful of graham cracker mixture in each muffin cup. Use a tiny glass to fill each cupcake liner with crumbs. Keep the extra graham cracker mixture aside for garnishing.
4. After that, place muffin pans in the oven and bake for approximately five minutes until the graham cracker mixture's edges turn brown. Take out from the oven.

Make the cupcakes

5. Mix sugar, flour, baking soda, baking powder, cocoa powder, and salt in a large bowl.
6. Whisk together eggs, milk, oil, and vanilla in a separate mixing bowl.
7. Whisk to blend after adding to the flour mixture.
8. Pour in the hot water and mix to blend. The mixture will be thin.
9. Pour batter into each muffin cup until three-quarters filled. Distribute the leftover graham cracker mixture evenly over each.
10. Back in the oven, bake for another 18-22 minutes, turning the pans halfway through, until the tops are set and a cake tester put in the center pulls out clean. Set muffin pans on a wire rack to cool for 10 minutes. Remove cupcakes from the pan and let to cool fully.

Make the frosting

11. Put the cream of tartar, sugar, and egg whites into the electric mixer's heatproof bowl. Place on top of a pot of simmering water. Whisk constantly for 3–5 minutes until sugar dissolves and whites are heated (160F).
12. Place the bowl in the electric mixer with the whisk attachment attached. Whisk for five to seven minutes, starting on medium speed and then rising to high, until firm, glossy peaks form. Mix in vanilla until well incorporated. Use immediately.
13. Spoon frosting into a big pastry bag and insert a large plain round or French tip into it. Pipe each cupcake with a spiral frosting design. Place the cupcakes onto a baking sheet. Lightly brown the frosting using a kitchen torch, being careful not to scorch the cupcake liners.
14. Lightly brown the frosting using a kitchen torch, being careful not to scorch the cupcake liners.
15. Add a delicious Hershey's square as a garnish (optional).

100. S'MORES COOKIE BARS

Prep Time: 10 Mins

Cook Time: 15 Mins

Total Time: 25 Mins

Servings: 24

Ingredients

Graham Cracker Crust

- 1¾ cups of graham cracker crumbs
- ¼ cup of granulated sugar
- ½ cup of melted butter (8 tbsp)

Cookie Dough

- 2 cups of all-purpose flour
- ½ tsp baking soda
- ½ tsp salt
- ¾ cup of unsalted butter, melted and slightly cooled
- 1 cup of packed brown sugar
- ½ cup of granulated sugar
- 1 tbsp vanilla extract
- 1 egg
- 1 egg yolk
- 1½ cups of semisweet chocolate chips
- 1½ cups of frozen mini-marshmallows
- 2 (1.55 oz) Hershey chocolate bars

Instructions

1. Set the oven's temperature to 350°F, or 165°C. Put marshmallows in the freezer (they freeze quickly). Apply cooking spray to a 9x13 baking dish.
2. For the crust made of graham crackers: Mix the butter, sugar, and crumbs together in a medium-sized bowl until well blended. Press mixture into baking dish.
3. After that, mix flour, baking soda, and salt in a sieve; set aside.

4. Ensure that the melted butter has cooled slightly before combining the brown sugar, white sugar, and cream in a medium-sized bowl until thoroughly combined. Beat until light and creamy after adding the egg, egg yolk, and vanilla. Add the sifted ingredients and stir until well combined. Incorporate one cup of frozen marshmallows and chocolate chips.

5. Spread the dough evenly over the graham cracker shell, pressing it down with a spoon. Fill the pan to the brim; the dough will bake over the entire contents. Press the remaining ½ cup of marshmallows slightly into the surface.

6. Bake for 18-25 minutes, until golden brown patches start to appear on top. Make sure the middle comes out of the oven completely firm, not jiggly. Take care not to overbake them as they will continue to solidify after cooling.

7. Once the bars are baked, take the pan out of the oven, let it cool for approximately five minutes, and then gently sprinkle the broken bits of candy bar on top. Allow to cool fully before slicing into squares.

101. OVEN-BAKED S'MORES

Total Time: 25 Mins

Servings: 4

Ingredients

- ½ cup of unsalted butter, cut into pieces
- ⅔ cup of packed light brown sugar
- ½ cup of 2% milk
- 1 tsp vanilla extract
- 1¼ cups of graham cracker crumb
- 350 g whole graham crackers (about 32-48, depends on the brand)
- 2½ cups of milk or semisweet chocolate chips
- 6 cups of mini marshmallows

Directions

1. Set oven temperature to 350°F. Then, cover an 8- or 9-inch square pan with parchment paper, leaving an inch above the edges.
2. Mix brown sugar, milk, and vanilla after melting butter in a skillet over medium-low heat; heat for one minute to de-chill the milk. Take out skillet from the heat and mix in the graham cracker crumbs to make a fluid paste.
3. After that, cover the bottom of the pan with graham crackers in a single layer. Spread a little amount (a third of the graham cracker paste—it doesn't have to cover the crackers entirely—over the layer of crumbs. Sprinkle a third of the marshmallows on top, then a third of the chocolate chips. Next, top this with another layer of graham crackers and repeat with the remaining third of paste, chocolate chips, and marshmallows. Repeat with the remaining chocolate chips, goo, crackers, and marshmallows.
4. Bake the marshmallows for 16 to 20 minutes, or until the tops are browned. If serving later, let the pan cool on a rack before chilling it all the way.
5. Divide the s'mores into squares; this is best to accomplish in the refrigerator. Serve now or keep at room temperature for three days.

102. S'MORES STUFFED COOKIES

Prep Time: 10 Mins

Total Time: 1 Hr 10 Mins

Servings: 8

Ingredients

For the Cookies

- 1¼ cups of (2 ½ sticks) softened butter
- ½ cup of granulated sugar
- 1 cup of packed brown sugar
- 2 tsp. pure vanilla extract
- 2 large eggs
- 2 ¾ cups of all-purpose flour
- 1 tsp. baking soda
- ¾ tsp. kosher salt
- 2 cups of semisweet chocolate chips

For the S'mores

- 8 graham crackers
- 8 marshmallows
- 3 (1.55-oz.) Hersheys bars, broken into squares of 4 pieces

Instructions

1. Set two big baking sheets with parchment paper on them and preheat the oven to 375º.
2. Prepare cookie dough: Using an electric mixer, whip the butter and sugars in a large bowl until they are light and fluffy, approximately 2 minutes. Add the eggs and vanilla essence gradually and beat until well combined.
3. After that, combine flour, baking soda, and salt in another bowl. Add chocolate chips and whisk until just mixed, then mix in butter-sugar mixture.
4. Construct S'mores Halve every marshmallow lengthwise. Place a halved marshmallow and a single slice of chocolate between two graham cracker squares. Repeat with the remaining ingredients for S'mores.

5. Put cookies together: Press ¼ cup of cookie dough into a circle slightly larger than the S'more. Place it on the ready baking sheet and top it with the S'more. After flattening and scooping out an additional ¼ cup of cookie dough, cover the S'more until no graham cracker is visible. Turn the cookie over so that the top scoop of dough is now exposed. Continue until all of the dough and s'mores have been utilized. On baking sheets, refrigerate for ten to fifteen minutes.
6. Bake for 16 to 18 minutes, until the cookies are gently brown. Before serving, let the baked goods to cool for ten minutes.

103. S'MORES DESSERT BOARD

Total Time: 10 Mins

Servings: 8

Ingredients

- 1 cup of chocolate chips
- ½ cup of mini M&Ms
- 1 sleeve ½ box graham crackers
- 2 chocolate bars
- ½ cup of chocolate-covered pretzels
- ½ cup of Reese's cups
- ½ cup of marshmallows
- ½ cup of strawberries
- ½ cup of cherries
- ½ cup of mini marshmallows

Instructions

1. Put your bowls on the board first. Generally, I advise placing your bowls on opposing sides to establish balance and ensure they occupy no more than ¼ of the board.
2. Then fill the bigger dish with chocolate chips and the smaller one with M&Ms.
3. It's time to get the board moving again!
4. Making a "S" shape with the graham crackers can help split the board and guide your eye across it.

5. Next, use huge clumps of your "large" components to fill up the empty area. For us, it was the fruit, chocolate bars, popcorn, and marshmallows. To make comparable pieces accessible from all sides, I prefer to place them opposite on the board. For instance, I arranged the chocolate bars and the chocolate-covered pretzels across from one another. The same goes for strawberries and cherries.

6. Finally, close any holes! I used mini marshmallows for this. You want to fill up any gaps to make the board seem full and bountiful!

7. Before serving, take pleasure in it immediately or keep it at room temperature for up to an hour!

104. S'MORES MILLIONAIRE BARS

Prep Time: 20 Mins

Total Time: 1 Hr 50 Mins

Servings: 6

Ingredients

For the Shortcake Layer

- ½ cup (1 stick) softened butter
- 3 tbsp. powdered sugar
- 1 tsp. pure vanilla extract
- 1½ cups of all-purpose flour
- ¼ cup of crushed graham cracker, plus more for garnish
- ¼ tsp. kosher salt

For the Caramel Layer

- 1 (11-oz.) package caramel squares
- ¼ cup of heavy cream

For the Marshmallow Layer

- ½ cup (1 stick) butter
- ¾ cup of marshmallow crème
- ¼ cup of powdered sugar
- Pinch kosher salt

For the Chocolate Layer

- 1 cup of semisweet chocolate chips
- 2 tbsp. butter
- Flaky sea salt, for garnish

Instructions

1. First, preheat oven to 350° and place parchment paper inside a 9" by 5" loaf pan.
2. Whisk butter and powdered sugar together in a large bowl with a hand mixer until well mixed. Stir in vanilla. Beat in the salt, graham cracker crumbs, and flour until well blended.
3. Press the shortbread dough into the loaf pan, and bake for approximately 20 minutes, or until gently brown. Allow to cool fully.
4. In the meanwhile, prepare the caramel layer: Melt the cream and caramels in a small saucepan over medium-low heat, stirring for 5 minutes. Drizzle over the chilled shortbread crust. While creating the marshmallow layer, refrigerate.
5. To make the marshmallow layer, combine marshmallow fluff and butter in a big dish and beat until frothy and light. Add the salt and powdered sugar, beating until smooth. Over the caramel layer, evenly distribute mixture. Freeze for 15 minutes.
6. Put butter and chocolate chips in a medium bowl that is safe to microwave. Now microwave on half power for 30 second intervals, stirring after each round, till the chocolate is smooth and melted. Over the marshmallow layer, spread evenly. Whisk in graham cracker crumbs and flaky sea salt and refrigerate until solid, 30 minutes.
7. Cut into 2-inch strips for serving. Maintain refrigeration.

105. OVEN BAKED S'MORES

Prep Time: 5 Mins

Cook Time: 2 Mins

Total Time: 7 Mins

Servings: 4

Ingredients

- 4 graham crackers, split in two
- 4 large marshmallows
- 1 Hershey's bar, divided into four equal pieces

Instructions

1. Place Graham Crackers onto a clean baking sheet.
2. Place a marshmallow on half of graham crackers.
3. Put some chocolate on the other half of the graham crackers.
4. Continue with the leftover Graham Crackers.
5. Bake them under broil for one to two minutes, monitoring closely as the marshmallows will go brown rapidly!
6. To make a s'more sandwich, match a chocolate bottom with a marshmallow top.
7. Enjoy while warm.

Notes

1. Make as many s'mores as you can fit on your cookie sheet!

106. COPYCAT STARBUCKS S'MORES FRAPPUCCINO

Total Time: 5 Mins

Servings: 1

Ingredients

- 1 cup of ice, ensure the ice is fresh
- 1 cup of milk of choice, for extra thick you can use half and half
- 1 shot espresso or, ½ cup of strong coffee Chilled before adding to recipe
- 2 tbsp chocolate syrup
- 1 tsp vanilla extract
- 1 ½ tbsp granulated sugar or vanilla syrup
- 1 (square) graham cracker
- 4 tbsp marshmallow cream
- 1 tsp milk of choice
- aerosol whipped cream for topping
- 1 to 2 tsp crushed graham crackers

Instructions

1. Prepare and cool your coffee or espresso before putting it to the blender with the remaining ingredients. Add 3 tbsp of the marshmallow cream with milk to a small microwave-safe bowl. Switch on for five seconds on medium power. Remove and mix. only to make the marshmallow cream softer. That is all. Disperse into the base of a tall glass or cup. Should you so want, you may slightly raise the sides. Pour some

of the chocolate syrup down the sides of the cup and over the cream. Give it a minute or so. Blend the other ingredients, including the cold coffee, at this point. But not the graham cracker crumbs or the whipped cream. Process everything on medium to high speed until everything is well blended and foamy. Add extra ice or vanilla ice cream to make the frappe thicker. Pour into cup, then swirl with whipped cream and sprinkle crumbled graham crackers over top. Insert a straw and take a drink!

107. S'MORES PANCAKES

Prep Time: 30 Mins

Cook Time: 10 Mins

Total Time: 40 Mins

Servings: 4

Ingredients

- 1 cup of all-purpose flour
- 1 tbsp granulated sugar
- 1 tbsp baking powder
- 1 tsp salt
- ¾ cup of graham cracker crumbs
- 1 large lightly beaten egg
- 2 tbsp melted unsalted butter
- 1¼ cups of milk of your choice
- ¼ cup of chocolate chips
- 1 batch Marshmallow Fluff (feel free to use store-bought Fluff or marshmallow sauce)
- 1 bar Hershey's Milk Chocolate

Homemade Marshmallow Fluff

- 2 large egg whites
- 1 cup of corn syrup
- ¼ tsp salt
- 1½ cups of confectioners' sugar
- 1 tbsp vanilla extract
- ¼ tsp cream of tarter

Instructions

1. Mix the flour, sugar, graham cracker crumbs, baking powder, and salt in a big bowl.
2. Mix the milk, melted butter, and whisked egg into the flour mixture until well combined. If there are still lumps, that's okay. Add chocolate chips and fold.
3. Next, coat a pan with a thin layer of cooking spray and heat it over medium heat. For each pancake, ladle roughly 3 tbsp of batter onto the griddle. Once you see bubbles forming on the pancakes, flip them and keep cooking until they get a golden-brown color.
4. Split the chocolate bar into pieces and place it in a double broiler or place it in a saucepan over another pot of boiling water, stirring to melt the chocolate.
5. To assemble: Drizzle a pancake with two to three tbsp of marshmallow fluff. Spread another two to three tbsp of fluff on top of the pancake. Continue with a third pancake, and then top with melted chocolate and more marshmallow fluff.
6. Garnish with miniature marshmallows, additional morsels of chocolate, or graham cracker crumbs, if desired. Enjoy!

Marshmallow Fluff

7. In a large bowl, use a hand mixer set to high speed to whisk the egg whites, corn syrup, and salt for about four to five minutes, until the mixture thickens considerably. The mixture will start off clear, but after pounding, it will become dazzling white.
8. Whisk in vanilla, cream of tartar, and confectioners' sugar at a moderate speed until blended.

108. S'MORES BANANA PUDDING

Total Time: 30 Mins

Servings: 4

Ingredients

- 1⅓ cups of whole milk
- 1 (3.9-oz.) package instant chocolate pudding mix
- 1 (14-oz.) can sweetened condensed milk
- 3 cups of heavy cream
- 1 cup of marshmallow fluff, microwaved for 10 seconds
- 1 tsp pure vanilla extract
- 3 cups of crushed graham crackers, plus quartered graham crackers for garnish

- 4 bananas, sliced into coins
- 3 Hershey's chocolate bars, broken into squares
- 2 cups of mini marshmallows

Instructions

1. Make pudding: Pour the milk, pudding mix, and sweetened condensed milk into a large mixing bowl. Mix well, breaking up any lumps, and chill for approximately five minutes, until it's set.
2. Make whipped cream: Combine vanilla, marshmallow fluff, and heavy cream in a separate, large bowl. Whisk with a hand mixer until firm peaks form.
3. Next, cover the bottom of a three-quart trifle dish with a few handfuls of crumbled graham crackers. Spread a third of the pudding on top, then cover with a layer of banana slices. Add half of the cream cheese. Add extra graham crackers, chocolate bars, and marshmallows on top. You could also want to arrange some of the crackers vertically so you can see the whole circle around the edge of the trifle dish.
4. Just one more layer of everything else, and then top it all off with whipped cream, chocolate bars, marshmallows, and graham crackers.
5. Refrigerate for at least three hours or up to overnight.

109. S'MORES KRISPIE TREATS

Prep Time: 10 Mins

Cook Time: 5 Mins

Total Time: 15 Mins

Servings: 18

Ingredients

- 6 tbsp salted butter
- 16oz bag mini marshmallows
- 6 cups of golden grahams cereal
- 1 cup of semi-sweet chocolate chips/chunks
- 4 snack size Hershey's Milk Chocolate Bars

Instructions

1. Apply cooking spray to a 9 x 13-inch baking dish. Set aside.
2. Place the cereal in a big bowl. Put the chocolate chips in. 3 cups of mini marshmallows should be taken out of the package. Combine 2½ cups of

marshmallows with the chocolate chips and cereal. Save the remaining ½ cup for later pressing into the top of the bars.

3. Melt the butter in a big saucepan over a medium-low heat. Add the leftover marshmallows. Stir continuously until the mixture just melts. Take off the heat. Allow it cool slightly for two minutes.

4. Cover the cereal mixture with the melted marshmallows. Mix until the coating is uniform. Then pour into prepared pan and smooth with a greased spatula or rolling pin.

5. Cut the Hershey's squares in half after separating them. Press the reserved ½ cup of mini marshmallows and the chocolate pieces into the top of the Krispie treats. TIP: Press or roll with a rolling pin after covering the surface with a layer of wax paper to reduce the sticky mess.

6. After fully cool, cut into squares and serve. Cover and keep any leftovers for up to five days at room temperature.

110. S'MORES COOKIE-DOUGH TRUFFLES

Prep Time: 10 Mins

Total Time: 35 Mins

Servings: 43

Ingredients

- 1½ cups of (3 sticks) softened butter
- 1½ cups of packed brown sugar
- 1 tbsp. pure vanilla extract
- 3¼ cups of crushed graham crackers, plus more for garnish
- 1 tsp. kosher salt
- ¾ cup of mini chocolate chips
- ¾ cup of marshmallow bits, plus more for garnish
- 3 cups of chocolate chips
- 1 ½ tbsp. coconut oil

Instructions

1. Cover a pair of tiny baking sheets with baking parchment. Whisk butter, brown sugar, and vanilla with an electric mixer in a large bowl till frothy and light. Add the salt and graham crackers, then mix in the little chocolate chips and marshmallow pieces.

2. Scoop the dough into tiny rounds and arrange them in a single layer on the baking pans using a small cookie scoop. Freeze for 15 minutes to harden.
3. Use 30 second bursts of microwave time to melt the chocolate chips while the truffle bites are still frozen. Combine the melted chocolate with the coconut oil and mix well.
4. Dip every truffle into the melted chocolate and mix until covered all over. Place back on baking sheet and immediately top with crumbled graham crackers and more marshmallow pieces.
5. Refrigerate or let sit for ten minutes until you're ready to serve.

111. BOOZY S'MORES MILKSHAKES

Total Time: 15 Mins

Servings: 1

Ingredients

For the dark chocolate fudge sauce

- ⅔ cup of heavy cream
- ½ cup of light corn syrup
- ½ cup of dark brown sugar, loosely packed
- 2 (3.2 ounce) bars chopped 70% dark chocolate
- 2 tsp vanilla extract
- 1 tbsp unsalted butter
- ¼ tsp salt

For the milkshake

- 1½ cups of chocolate ice cream
- ½ cup of vanilla ice cream
- 1 graham cracker "sheet", plus extra crushed graham crackers for riming the glass
- 2 toasted marshmallows, plus extra for garnish
- 1 ½ ounces coffee liquor
- ½ cup of whole milk
- 2 tbsp dark chocolate fudge sauce
- honey for riming the glass
- whipped cream for topping, optional
- extra chopped dark chocolate for topping, optional

Instructions

Dark chocolate fudge sauce

1. Mix the brown sugar, heavy cream, light corn syrup, and half of the chopped chocolate in a medium saucepan. Bring to a boil and whisk to melt the chocolate for two to three minutes. (Make careful not to boil the mixture—it will separate and get gritty.) Take off the heat and whisk in the remaining chocolate, butter, vanilla, and salt until well combined. Allow to cool fully before blending milkshakes.

Milkshake

2. Press the smashed graham crackers firmly to cling to the honey rim of the goblet. Blend together the chocolate, vanilla, and graham cracker ice creams, toasted marshmallows, coffee liquor, milk, and dark chocolate fudge sauce in a blender. Blend till creamy and smooth. Pour into glass and top with chopped dark chocolate, crumbled graham crackers, whipped cream, and a toasted marshmallow for decoration. Enjoy immediately!

112. DEEP-DISH S'MORES SKILLET COOKIE

Prep Time: 15 Mins

Total Time: 1 Hr 30 Mins

Servings: 10

Ingredients

- ¾ cup of graham cracker crumbs
- 1 cup of semisweet chocolate chips
- 2 packages (16 oz) refrigerated chocolate chip cookie dough (24 Count)
- ¾ cup of miniature marshmallows

Instructions

1. Preheat oven to 350°F.
2. Pour ¾ cup of graham cracker crumbs into the bottom of a 9-inch ovenproof pan or cast-iron. Sprinkle about 2 tbsp of the 1 cup of semisweet chocolate chips over the cracker crumbs.
3. Crumble one box of cookie dough with your fingers into the pan. Sprinkle about ⅓ cup of the leftover chocolate chips over the first layer of cookie dough.

4. Add crumbled cookie dough from the second box on top. Add a final ⅓ cup of chocolate chips.
5. Bake for an hour. Take the skillet out of the oven. Adjust the oven to broil.
6. Place the remaining chocolate chips and ¾ cup of small marshmallows on top of the heated cookie. Heat the pan under the broiler until the marshmallows start to puff up and get a light golden color. Before serving heated, let it cool somewhat, 5 to 10 minutes.

113. S'MORES ICEBOX CAKE

Prep Time: 25 Mins

Chill Time: 4 Hrs

Total Time: 4 Hr 25 Mins

Servings: 20

Ingredients

- 2½ cups of chocolate chips
- 2 cups of heavy cream
- 16 oz whipped topping thawed
- 7-ounce marshmallow fluff
- 2 cups of mini marshmallows
- 14.4-ounces graham crackers

For garnish

- Extra marshmallows, graham crackers and chocolate chunks

Instructions

Make the Ganache

1. Put the chocolate chips into a bowl.
2. Heat heavy cream in a small saucepan till boiling.
3. Pour cream over the chocolate and let it remain for a few minutes before stirring until melted and creamy.
4. Refrigerate while you prepare the other ingredients.

For the Cake

5. Mix the marshmallow fluff, marshmallows, and whipped topping in a big bowl.
6. Coat the base of a 13 by 9-inch pan lightly. This just holds the cracker layer in place.
7. Toss in some graham crackers. Use size-appropriate crackers to cover any voids.
8. Spread an equal layer of ⅓ of the marshmallow mixture on top.
9. Add half of the chocolate ganache after that.
10. Repeat with graham crackers, ⅓ marshmallow mixture, and the remaining ganache.
11. Place the last layer of graham crackers and the last third of the marshmallow mixture on top.
12. For at least four hours or overnight, cover and chill.
13. Now add marshmallows, chocolate chunks, and graham cracker crumbs as garnish if preferred.

114. MINI S'MORES TARTS

Total Time: 2 Hr

Servings: 48

Ingredients

For Crust

- ½ box (12 cookies) finely chopped graham crackers (about 1½ cups of crumbs)
- 1 tbsp brown sugar
- 5 tbsp melted unsalted butter

For Chocolate Layer

- 12 ounces chopped dark chocolate
- 12 ounces chopped milk chocolate
- 1 cup of heavy cream

For Marshmallow Topping

- 2 ¼ tsp unflavored gelatin (from 1 packet)
- ½ cup of cold water, divided
- ¾ cup of granulated sugar
- ½ cup of corn syrup, divided
- ½ tsp vanilla extract

Directions

1. Set oven temperature to 350°F. Use paper liners to line two 24-count mini cupcake tins.
2. Add sugar to the graham cracker crumbs to make the crust. Add the butter and whisk with a fork when the mixture resembles wet sand. Using a regular size shot glass, this process is ideal and much less laborious than using your fingers. Put a half spoonful of the crumble mixture onto the bottom of each muffin pan. Press down firmly. Bake for 4 to 5 minutes, or until the crust sets. Allow to cool.
3. Put cream and chopped chocolates into a saucepan. Whisk over low heat until smooth and melted chocolate has formed. Pour the chocolate mixture into each cup, filling it close to the brim. Gently tap pans on the counter to flatten the surface and eliminate air bubbles. Refrigerate for at least one hour or overnight until set.
4. Combine ¼ cup of cold water for the marshmallow topping in a separate bowl. After scattering the gelatin over, let it to soften for five minutes.
5. Put ¼ cup of corn syrup, ¼ cup of water, and the remaining ¼ cup of sugar into a small pot. Over medium-high heat, boil, stirring regularly, and continue boiling until the mixture reads 240 degrees Fahrenheit on a candy thermometer.
6. Transfer the remaining ¼ cup of corn syrup into the stand mixer bowl. Add gelatin mixture to the corn syrup bowl after heating it for 5 to 10 seconds on high, or until it is fully melted. Decrease the mixer speed and gradually pour in the heated sugar syrup. After adding all the syrup, mix the mixer to medium-high and mix for five minutes. Add the vanilla essence and beat on high speed for 5 minutes until the marshmallow is opaque, glossy, and quadrupled in volume.
7. Place the marshmallow in a piping bag with a big round tip. Spoon generous amounts of marshmallow onto every tart. Allow the marshmallow to rest for 20 to 30 minutes. Then, using a kitchen torch or the broiler, carefully toast the marshmallow for a few seconds until it becomes golden brown, taking care not to burn the parchment paper. Once again, place the chocolate in the refrigerator for a minimum of thirty minutes to solidify. Tarts are stored well in the refrigerator for up to two days. However, they are best eaten the day they are prepared.

115. S'MORES COFFEE CAKE

Prep Time: 20 Mins

Cook Time: 1 Hr

Total Time: 1 Hr 20 Mins

Servings: 20

Ingredients

Coffee Cake Batter

- 2½ cups of all-purpose flour
- 1 cup of granulated sugar
- 1 tsp. baking soda
- ½ tsp. salt
- 1 ½ sticks unsalted butter, sliced into chunks
- 2 large eggs
- 2 egg yolks
- 2 tsp. vanilla extract
- ⅔ cup of buttermilk
- ¼ cup of cocoa powder

Streusel

- ⅓ cup of granulated sugar
- ⅔ cup of brown sugar
- 1 ½ tsp. cinnamon
- ¼ tsp. salt
- 2 sticks melted butter
- 1½ cups of flour
- ¼ cup of chocolate chips
- ¼ cup of mini marshmallows

Directions

1. Start the oven to 325 degrees Fahrenheit. Grease a loaf pan.
2. **Make batter:** Combine the flour, sugar, baking soda, and salt in a large bowl. Add the butter, one piece at a time, beating until crumbles the size of peas appear. Whisk in the buttermilk, cocoa powder, vanilla extract, and eggs and yolks. Whisk for another two minutes or until smooth.

3. **Prepare the streusel:** Combine sugar, butter, flour, cinnamon, brown sugar, salt, and chocolate chips in a big bowl. Mix with your hands after combining until crumbles start to form. Sprinkle streusel over batter.
4. Bake for 40 minutes, then top with little marshmallows. After 15 to 20 minutes, until a toothpick inserted into the middle pulls out clean, continue baking. Allow to cool fully.

116. EASY CARAMEL APPLE S'MORES

Total Time: 46 Mins

Servings: 4

Ingredients

- 12 graham crackers
- 2 granny smith apples, sliced ¼ inch thick
- 6 marshmallows
- caramel sauce

Instructions

1. Toast marshmallows first (ideally over a campfire). Then, place the roasted marshmallow on a graham cracker.
2. Over the marshmallow, drizzle some caramel.
3. Place a piece of apple on top and cover it with more caramel.
4. Top with a graham cracker to create a sandwich.

117. S'MORES CRUNCHWRAP

Prep Time: 20 Mins

Cook Time: 1 Hr

Total Time: 1 Hr 20 Mins

Servings: 20

Ingredients

- 2 large flour tortillas
- ¾ cup of marshmallows
- 1 Hershey's chocolate bar
- 1 roll Ritz Crackers or Graham Crackers
- 1 tbsp butter
- 4 tbsp granulated sugar
- 1 ½ tbsp cinnamon

Instructions

1. First, combine the sugar and cinnamon; transfer to a shallow plate and reserve.
2. After that, warm a pan over medium heat and add butter, allowing it to melt.
3. Place the marshmallows in the middle of each tortilla once you've laid them out.
4. Add some crackers on top, followed by the chocolate.
5. Continue by covering another layer of crackers.
6. Next, make folds by rolling the edges into the middle of the tortilla.
7. After that, put the tortilla face down in the big skillet and toast it for two to three minutes, or until it turns golden brown.
8. Turn the tortilla over and continue with the other side.
9. Take the tortilla off of the burner and coat both sides with the cinnamon-sugar mixture. Next, serve it hot.

118. PEANUT BUTTER CUP S'MORES

Total Time: 30 Mins

Servings: 4

Ingredients

- Graham crackers or gluten-free graham crackers
- Peanut butter cups
- Marshmallows

Instructions

1. Heat the marshmallow over an open flame with a stick until it browns and melts.
2. Half a graham cracker should have a marshmallow on it.
3. Place the peanut butter cup and the remaining cracker half on top.

119. S'MORES CHEESE BALL

Total Time: 10 Mins

Servings: 1

Ingredients

S'mores Cheese Ball Mixture

- 2 pkgs cream cheese (8 oz. each)
- ½ cup of powdered sugar
- ½ cup of marshmallow cream
- ⅓ cup of mini marshmallows
- ⅓ cup of mini chocolate chips
- ½ tsp vanilla (optional)
- pinch of coarse/kosher salt

Smore's Ball Topping

- 5 whole crushed graham crackers
- ⅓ cup of mini chocolate chips
- ½ cup of mini marshmallows

Cookie/Cracker Suggestions for dipping

- graham crackers
- Nilla Wafers
- animal crackers/cookies
- shortbread cookies
- teddy grahams

Instructions

1. In a medium-sized bowl, combine the cream cheese, marshmallow cream, powdered sugar, kosher salt, and optional vanilla. Mix ingredients using a hand mixer with a paddle attachment. Blend until well combined.
2. Mix in the little chocolate chips and marshmallows until thoroughly combined. It's optional to add little chocolate chips and marshmallows to the cheese ball. You can omit this step if you want the cheese ball to be smooth enough for dipping. You may adjust the amount of them, if you decide to add them, to suit your taste.
3. To make the cream cheese mixture more solid to form into a ball, refrigerate it in the refrigerator for 20 to 30 minutes.
4. As the cheese ball cools, break apart the graham crackers and arrange them in a shallow dish. Mix thoroughly after adding the little marshmallows and chocolate chips. The cheese ball will be rolled in this mixture, allowing you to add as much or as few chocolate chips and little marshmallows as your little heart wishes.
5. Form cream cheese mixture into a ball when it has cooled in the refrigerator. The ball should then be uniformly coated all over with the S'mores topping mixture by rolling it in it.
6. Serve the cheese ball with your preferred cookies and crackers. There are just two days this cheese ball will last in the refrigerator. The longer it rests, the graham crackers in the topping will get softer.

120. S'MORES PUMPKIN CUPCAKES

Prep Time: 15 Mins

Total Time: 45 Mins

Servings: 12

Ingredients

- 3 cups of graham cracker crumbs, plus more for garnish
- 12 tbsp. melted butter
- 2 tbsp. sugar
- pinch of kosher salt
- 1 box vanilla cake mix plus ingredients listed on the box
- 1 (15-oz.) can pumpkin purée
- 1 (11-oz.) bag chocolate chips
- ¾ cup of heavy cream
- 12 marshmallows

Instructions

1. Preheat the oven to 350°. Cover a 12-cup muffin tray with cupcake liners.
2. In the meantime, mix together the butter, sugar, salt, and graham cracker crumbs in a small bowl. Press about 1 spoonful of the mixture into each cupcake liner to form small crusts.
3. Combine the canned pumpkin and vanilla cake mix in a large mixing bowl. Pour batter over graham cracker crusts.
4. Put the cupcakes in the oven and bake for 22 minutes, until a toothpick put into one comes out clean.
5. Slightly chill while preparing the ganache: Fill a heat-resistant dish with chocolate chips. Whisk the heavy cream in a small saucepan and bring to a boil over low heat. Whisk till smooth after pouring over chocolate chunks and letting them stand for two minutes.
6. Place a tbsp of ganache on top of each cupcake, allowing some to drip down the edges. Top with a marshmallow and put back in the oven. Bake for another five minutes or until the marshmallow becomes brown.
7. Add graham cracker crumbs as a garnish.

THE END

Made in the USA
Las Vegas, NV
18 December 2024